HEARTY

Also by andrea bennett

the berry takes the shape of the bloom

Canoodlers

Like a Boy but Not a Boy:
Navigating Life, Mental Health, and
Parenthood Outside the Gender Binary

Moon Montréal

Moon Québec City

Points of Interest
(co-edited with David Beers)

HEARTY

On Cooking, Eating, and Growing
Food for Pleasure and Subsistence

ESSAYS

andrea bennett

Published by ECW Press
665 Gerrard Street East
Toronto, Ontario, Canada M4M 1Y2
416-694-3348 / info@ecwpress.com

Editor for the Press: Jen Knoch
Copy-editor: Crissy Boylan
Cover design: Jessica Albert
Author photo: Erin Flegg

LIBRARY AND ARCHIVES CANADA CATALOGUING
IN PUBLICATION

Title: Hearty : on cooking, eating, and growing
food for pleasure and subsistence / andrea bennett.

Names: bennett, andrea (Author of Canoodlers)

Identifiers: Canadiana (print) 20240354613 |
Canadiana (ebook) 20240354656

ISBN 978-1-77041-760-1 (softcover)
ISBN 978-1-77852-308-3 (ePub)
ISBN 978-1-77852-316-8 (PDF)

Subjects: LCSH: Food habits. | LCSH: Food—
Social aspects. | LCSH: Cooking. | LCSH:
Vegetable gardening.

Classification: LCC GT2850 .B46 2024 | DDC
394.1/2—dc23

This book is funded in part by the Government of Canada. *Ce livre est financé en partie par le gouvernement du
Canada.* We acknowledge the support of the Canada Council for the Arts. *Nous remercions le Conseil des arts du
Canada de son soutien.* We would like to acknowledge the funding support of the Ontario Arts Council (OAC) and
the Government of Ontario for their support. We also acknowledge the support of the Government of Ontario
through the Ontario Book Publishing Tax Credit, and through Ontario Creates.

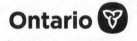

PRINTED AND BOUND IN CANADA   PRINTING: MARQUIS   5 4 3 2 1

For Kim

contents

introduction   ix

1. illness and appetite   1

2. two bags of lettuce   12

3. tomato chutney, part i: reviving my nana's recipe   32

4. tomato chutney, part ii: the empire in a sandwich   39

5. because someone saved the seed   51

6. vegan lemon macawrongs   66

7. the spins family board game   77

8. consider the carrot   85

9. on substitution   98

10. the garden will bloom again   109

11. a fifty-pound bag of potatoes   116

12. the spectacle of the big bite   133

13. trifling   142

14. the failure of the peppers   154

15. give us this day our daily beans   166

16. a taste for finery   173

17. twenty-four batches of ice cream   182

18. pestilence and abundance   200

acknowledgements   211

endnotes   212

introduction

O n the way to school last year, my then-five-year-old Sinclair
often threaded through a small stand of evergreens on the
lawn of an empty house—to a kindergartener, the trees felt like
a magical forest. The house had been empty and for sale since
the previous spring, during lilac season, when I availed myself of
the blooms of a bush between the evergreens and the sidewalk
to make lilac simple syrup.

When new people finally moved in, I told Sinclair she'd need
to stop crossing the lawn. "It's private property," I explained.
"There are people living there now."

One afternoon, Sinclair went through the trees again and we
were repeating our conversation about other people's lawns when
a voice piped up: "She can cross through if she wants!" Our new
neighbour said hello and we chatted briefly. When I confessed
I'd harvested her lilacs last year when the house was empty, she
encouraged me to pick them again this year. And so I brought a
metal bowl and a pair of secateurs to school drop-off one morning, and on my way home, I snipped until the bowl was filled
with clusters of purple flowers.

"I use them for simple syrup," I told her. "And then to make
lemonade."

And that's what I did: after work, I plucked the flowers from the branches while listening to Nirvana. Once they were all cleanly separated from the stems, I washed them under cold water in a fine-mesh sieve. I mixed equal parts sugar and water in a pot, bringing it to a boil, added the flowers to simmer at the end for a minute, and then steeped them overnight on the countertop. The next day, I strained out the flowers. When we walked to school, I left a not-quite-full Bonne Maman jam jar of the syrup on a chair by my neighbour's door with a recipe for lilac lemonade: one part syrup, one part lemon juice, two parts water.

The lilac syrup itself is one of the most inviting things I've ever consumed. Drinking it feels like something out of *Alice's Adventures in Wonderland*: for the briefest of moments, I get to be *inside* the vibrant fragrance of the lilac, transformed. I imagine this is what a bumblebee feels like every day. If made with purple lilacs (and not a white variety), the syrup is a beautiful light violet. And the lemonade is pink—the result of the anthocyanins in the lilac flowers reacting with the acid in the lemons.

I was describing lilac lemonade to Sinclair's kindergarten teacher that week while we were making latkes with the class, and we realized that it would be a fun activity to do with the kids. With permission, I gathered lilacs from another neighbour's house, leaving a couple kale seedlings on the picnic table in their yard as a thank you.

In the classroom that Friday, a dozen tiny hands worked to pull the flowers from the branches. But it was the day before the May long weekend; everything descended into chaos, and we had to cut things short. The kids filed out, and I finished up the syrup in the quiet of the cafeteria, with the intermittent cacophony normal to an elementary school dopplering through the halls.

I share these anecdotes not because they're exceptional but because they're illustrative: I love to grow food, to cook food, to talk about food (where people in town are finding good cheese;

who's doing the next bulk order for beans or nuts or spices; how our region could support more farms). It's often the primary way I'm in community with friends and acquaintances where I live. Seed swapping by mail or making a loved one's recipe, I remain in community with friends and acquaintances and family who live elsewhere.

The connections I make this way are often small and simple. Sometimes they build into something bigger over time, and sometimes they don't. Sometimes what seems like a good idea—making lilac syrup with kids—works out the way it might on a television segment, or Pinterest, but more often it's imperfect, and sometimes it completely slides off the rails.

In these food-centric interactions with friends and loved ones and kids and neighbours, there's space to be experimental and creative while also being nourished and practical. It's all pretty low-stress. We eat things, and we love them or hate them or find them fine enough, and then they're gone. The process of eating several times a day helps with this—like an endless ocean of waves breaking on the beach.

When we eat, cook, and grow food, we are implicated in cycles of birth and germination and harvest. In community, in pleasure. For me, it is a way to be grounded and connected, to participate directly in life. To nudge free of nuclear family structures and seek ones that are more supportive, less capitalistic.

I often feel quite anxious about the world, worrying about climate change and drought and soil erosion and running out of the fossil fuels that ship our foods and create our fertilizers. But when I participate in these life cycles, and connect with others who are working to seek solutions to these problems, my anxieties, like my hunger, can be temporarily allayed.

Food has been a big part of my life for decades now, though it hasn't always been as charming as lilac lemonade. Starting in my teens, I spent ten years working in food service. I worked at an organic bakery; I worked at a Subway. I worked a small-town salad bar; I worked at Tim Hortons; I worked at a curry restaurant and at a well-known vegetarian restaurant in Guelph, Ontario, that made everything from scratch. During parts of this period, I was involved in a tenants' union that cooked free meals and wrote letters to help fellow tenants fight evictions and force their landlords to fix issues with their rental suites. I was often poor and overworked. And mentally ill—I'm bipolar and have generalized anxiety disorder.

My life experiences mean I'm not interested in personal judgments about what people eat or how they eat it. The strictures of life, alongside the particular cultures in which we're raised, shape what makes it onto our plates. It makes very little sense to expect individuals to solve problems that have their roots in structural issues.

Our bodies need sustenance; our budgets determine what we can afford; our schedules determine how much time we have to devote to cooking. Meals, often social, provide opportunities for cultural connection—and sometimes opportunities for anxiety, if you have allergies, sensory issues, or a complicated relationship with food. We might need to make what other people might consider a bad decision, like extracting the last of what's left on a credit card to buy a veggie burger combo from Harvey's—providing an opt-out from making dinner, alongside a nice little hit of dopamine from crunching into the onion rings. (Ask me why this example is so specific.)

I'm much more interested in exploring how things could be functioning better, in ways that are equitable, support labourers, meet people where they are, recognize the interiority and autonomy of animals, stop borrowing resources from the future, and do not further enrich millionaires and billionaires—they've extracted enough from us.

I think about food systems like I think about public transit: people make the best decisions they can in the circumstances in which they find themselves, and if I'm worrying about climate change and labour justice, and concerned about animal welfare, then the best way to seek change is at the systems level. It would be great if everyone took the bus, but if the bus isn't accessible, doesn't run where you need it to go, and costs too much, ridership won't go up. The fixes are easier for transit. What might they look like for food?

When I cook, I make hearty food. For subsistence but, just as importantly, for pleasure. To keep myself alive and to enrich my life. My goal was to approach these essays from the same place I approach gardening, harvesting, and cooking—with curiosity, with optimism, and in community.

What you won't find is much, if any, admonition about the consumption of beef or high-fructose corn syrup. No recommendation to eat food, not too much, mostly plants.

Instead, I hope that sharing some of what I've been thinking about as I research and write and live and make lilac lemonade might be a way to extend the conversations I've been having with friends and family and cooks and farmers.

And so, in the pages ahead, I'll combine journalism, cookery, and some horticulture in order to study the local and the systemic, the personal and the cultural, aiming to understand where we're coming from and where we could head next. I'll figure out why my grandfather's carrots tasted so different from the cello-packed supermarket version, trace the journey of lettuce from seed in

Arizona to my home in B.C., mull over my family history of heart disease while making ice cream with berries and herbs from my yard, and try to heal myself from perfectionism while volunteering at a local farm.

Eating is one of the most important things almost every living being does on a daily basis. Our eating habits are shaped by personal and global forces long before we're born, even as what we eat now is shaping the future. I think the best way to change our food systems is to tap into the pleasure we derive from eating in a way that's conscious of colonialism and community and cultural roots, that meets us where we are but inspires us to seek alternatives that might better sustain us all. To eat a heap of broccoli not instead of a box of Kraft Dinner but in addition to it, because when we can access greens, and roast them with oil and salt, they're delicious.

illness and appetite

"Vegetarians are the enemy of everything good and
decent in the human spirit, an affront to all I stand
for, the pure enjoyment of food."
—ANTHONY BOURDAIN, *Kitchen Confidential*

When Anthony Bourdain speaks disdainfully of vegetarians
in *Kitchen Confidential*, writing that they are "a persistent
irritant to any chef worth a damn," it feels deeply short-sighted.
"Life without veal stock, pork fat, sausage, organ meat, demi-glace
or even stinky cheese," he continues, "is a life not worth living."
He'll accommodate vegetarians, he writes, if he has to—"fourteen
dollars for a few slices of grilled eggplant and zucchini suits my
food cost fine."

There is a lot to like about Bourdain's approach to eating and
cooking and the culture of kitchens. But his approach to feeding
vegetarians signals less that vegetables are so dull they should
be an afterthought, but rather that when vegetables are treated as
an afterthought, they become dull.

When chefs scorn people like me—people who opt not to
eat much meat, people who have other dietary restrictions, like

gluten or dairy or nuts—I think about what experiences we miss out on because someone in the kitchen finds us irritating. And I think about the extent to which constraints can be the basis of creativity.

Beans and grains and fruits and vegetables are worthy of the same thoughtful treatment with which chefs prepare everything else. Why, at least in mainstream North America, is pleasure treated as the providence of meat?

And why is writing about vegetarianism[1] so often aligned with a weird sort of health and environmental purity culture? I have little desire to be proselytized to about food, which is so often what's on offer in books that make the case for eating vegetables. I have absolutely no desire—working at *Adbusters* as a plump person extinguished it completely[2]—to hear about how ignorant fat people eating McDonald's are the root of all the world's ills.

Where are all the bestselling essay collections obsessed with tomatoes and seaweed and ginger and white beans and butter and herbs?

When I was nine, I stopped eating red meat. My most constant friend was my cat, a domestic shorthair named Cinnamon whose

---

1   That is, essays and commentary—not cookbooks. There are a lot of great vegetarian cookbooks.

2   One commonly used *Adbusters* image features a man with a large belly wearing suspenders. On a 2008 cover, issue 80, an iteration of this image is paired with the text "Freedom isn't free. This is abuse of the freedom from want." Another shows two headless bodies, both with large bellies—one fat, and one from famine—with the sarcastic cutline "No connection." Issue 83 featured Henrich Kimerling's *American Beauty*—a photo of a fat woman wearing a bikini, surrounded by convenience foods—on a spread that reads "GLUTTONY" on the opposite page.

warm brown undercoat shimmered in the sunlight under his soft black fur. Cinnamon, who feared my unpredictable mother as much as I did, sought me out when I was upset. He slept on my bed, curled up on my lap, purred in something close to sympathy.

Until we got Cinnamon, I hadn't spent much time considering the farm-to-slaughterhouse-to-grocery-store relationship between animals and meat. We fished, but I didn't know anyone who hunted; no one brought venison to our house. Looking at Cinnamon one day flipped a switch: there was no real difference, other than our personal connection, between him and any given cow or pig.

Red meat must have been a compromise with my parents; it may even have been palatable to my image-obsessed mother, considering that I was a chubby child in the low-fat '90s. But then at twelve, I stopped eating chicken and fish too. My mother, who generally fed us, viewed this as mutiny.

So I learned how to cook.

There are many ways to find pleasure in vegetarian food. You can extract it, through techniques like braising and infusing and by using rich blends of herbs and spices. You can keep things simple; add a chiffonade of mint to grilled peach and ricotta toast at the height of summer. You can spend heaps of money on fancy cheese, or much less money on beans and pulses and alliums, or meet in the middle—buying a few spendy things like parmesan and avocados to round out cheaper meals. (Where you live and what's easily available to you, of course, plays a role in determining this; it might be easier to grow avocados than broccoli, eggplants than carrots.)

What I first learned to cook in the '90s in white suburban Ontario, with no computer and no cable TV, were stir-fries and curries. Both were basically pan-Asian, and I relied on prepared sauces—Patak's and store-brand jars of teriyaki shaped like salad dressings. Instead of choosing a few complementary vegetables for any given dish, I added a small amount of everything I had in the fridge. I undersalted, timed things poorly, burned my rice, cut my carrots into too-thick coins and overcooked them. I had to use a small dull knife for everything. I ate a lot of canned soup and beans on toast.

Then I started working in kitchens—prep at Tim Hortons, the salad bar at my best friend's father's produce store. These kitchens had large knives, sharp peelers; I quickly learned that there was an order in which one did things. That salad dressing needed far more oil than I'd initially thought. That to make food taste good, it was necessary to balance salt and sweet and fat and acid. Mushrooms, which we only ate raw in salad at home and which I thought had the texture of packing peanuts, became one of my favourite-ever foods when cooked in butter in an uncrowded skillet.

Ripe pineapple, not from the can, was another revelation. I ate whatever I could get my hands on. And I came to love prep work: each fruit and vegetable calling for its own way to be broken down with a knife, lined up until it was ready for the gentle thwack-thwack-thwack of the blade onto the cutting board. I had always enjoyed eating sweet carrots straight from my grandfather's garden. I liked the subtleness of cucumbers and the thirst-quenching greenness of the celery my nana cut and kept in water-filled cups in the fridge. Working in food let me taste more. The salad bar began to teach me how to approach a fistful of vegetables and make them into dozens of dishes, each with its own distinct flavours and textures. Vegetables contained multitudes.

At sixteen, I was at my friend Jenny's apartment, helping her make a Thai curry with tofu for dinner. Jenny lived with her dad in an apartment above a business downtown. We set cutting boards up on an island, or peninsula, in the kitchen, and prepped the vegetables together. Jenny used green curry paste and coconut milk and lemongrass. She cut the bottoms off the lemongrass, smashed them, and stuck them in the pot with the paste and vegetables and some water. I'd never eaten green curry, and the flavours—in particular, the perfume of the lemongrass—lit a little sparkler in my brain. Jenny taught me how to make it, and I started making it myself at home. Dish by dish, ingredient by ingredient, I learned to make what I wanted to eat.

My turn away from vegetarianism began with the removal of my gallbladder in my early twenties. After initially being misdiagnosed—a doctor at my school's health clinic took one look at my chart, saw "anxiety," and turned me away as if I had nothing more than a nervous tummy—I lived with gallstone attacks for months. After I finally had surgery, the attacks stopped, but I never fully got better. For a while, I kept eating as though everything would eventually be okay. I saw another doctor, who didn't notice anything amiss, other than anemia. Things progressed; I began to double over after eating or feel a need to lie down with my knees tucked into my stomach, waiting for the pain to pass. My body stopped sending hunger cues. I started feeling full after eating just a few tentative bites. And then I started to fear eating, knowing it would bring pain.

Eventually, the doctor suggested I see a naturopath, and the naturopath suggested an elimination diet. After eliminating a lot of different foods, I stopped feeling so sick after I ate. But the list of what I had to avoid was long: gluten, peanut butter, all dairy other than yogurt, and basically anything high fat made me feel sick. I could stomach things like corn tortillas and eggs, steamed vegetables and almond butter.

I lost so much weight that my grandmother, who had lived through rationing in the wake of the Second World War, grew concerned. But having received both cultural messages and messages from my mother that my larger body made me undesirable and signalled that I was weak-willed, I was not concerned. Initially, in fact, I felt like I'd discovered the key to success: my body, now so bad at digestion, no longer seemed to want me to feed it.

But I did get shaky. And I had to Lego together nutritional blocks of meals with only one-quarter of the set. When I exercised, instead of feeling strong, I felt a giant weight pressing on my chest. Biking against the wind one day, something my friends were managing well enough, I felt so weak and unable to keep up, I began to cry. I stopped menstruating.

The food restrictions I was living with made it hard to go out to eat with friends or grab something while I was out running errands. Then, like now, I walked and biked everywhere; if I got stuck in the middle of nowhere without an adequate meal or snack, I became seized with panic. Like my grandmother had foreseen, my body no longer had anything to fall back on. No reserves.

I also began, eventually, to worry about how much control and caution I was exerting over what appeared on my plate. Most of that caution was necessary, but it had also activated the part of my brain that had been trained to hate and control my physical appearance. As a child and teen, it was my hunger, my body's desire for life and strength, that encouraged me to eat instead of starving myself to be smaller. But my weakened body couldn't advocate for itself. I needed my mind to let go of the idea of being thin, as accidental as the road to thinness had initially been.

When I chose to add chicken and fish and bacon and steak back into my diet, it felt like I was choosing between my own self-preservation and that of the animals I'd be eating.

I chose my own self-preservation.

Three decades later, that fundamental truth I felt about Cinnamon still feels true, even though I eat meat once or twice a month. Animals are autonomous beings with their own personalities and understandings of the world, and it seems odd to categorize them based on whether or not they're inclined to develop personal relationships with humans, to culturally separate them into pet and not pet. Often when people propose thought experiments on these questions, they'll contrast North American cultural understandings of animals with another culture's understandings—but that's not actually necessary. What I've always found fascinating are our very own homegrown boundary cases. I love bunnies, for example, identifying with their anxiety and their mischievous love of raw vegetables and their tendency to stomp their powerful hind legs when alerting or angry. Some people keep rabbits as pets, and some people eat them, and that's not a clean split. While my pet bunnies roamed my house, nibbling on my paperbacks and being fed like petite feted kings, lots of people keep them in pens outdoors, caring for them before harvesting them for the table. Some North Americans view horses as pets, and some view horses as dinner. Some keep frogs, and some eat them. No one would bat at an eye at a parrot owner eating a chicken salad sandwich.

It's my decision about what to *do* with the information that animals are thinking, feeling beings that has changed. I see vegetarianism as only one of the conclusions a person could come to, and I see my vegetarianism as having been deeply influenced by my culture, upbringing, and surroundings. Another equally valid conclusion would be that humans are more similar to other animals than some of us might believe, and as omnivores, it's pretty natural to participate in the food chain by eating other animals. Just because I grew up in the suburbs and ate industrially produced meat doesn't mean that's everyone's relationship to eating animals. Further, even if it is, meat is a calorically dense vehicle for protein and fat. When your budget is tight, an on-sale cut stored in the freezer can go a long way, making meals feel satisfying and keeping you satiated longer.

If animals are thinking, feeling beings and humans are still going to eat them, because we are animals and we like meat, one addressable problem is that of animal welfare: to offer the animals we farm a better life. This is the solution that Eliza MacLean, an animal rescuer turned pig farmer in North Carolina, has opted for. "I have spent my life finding, receiving, injured animals," she tells the filmmakers of *Cooked*, the Netflix series inspired by Michael Pollan's book. "Once I decided that I could raise animals, which I'd been saving my whole life, to be food, I really wanted, even more, for them to have the best life that they could, and be themselves." MacLean even runs a stewardship camp to teach youth about farming and our responsibility to the land.

Another solution is to rely more on sustainably harvested wild animals—an ancestral right of Indigenous Peoples on this continent that needs to be prioritized above settler hunting rights, as colonial plunder has endangered the habitats of so many animal species.

And yet another solution is a cultural shift, one that could come directly from the chefs people watch on television and see in magazines. Just as HGTV exalts unnecessary, expensive renovations as the world is burning, so does the Food Network centre its entire aspirational ethos around cuts of meat.

Watch any competitive cooking show—from *Iron Chef* to *Chopped* to *Top Chef*—and it will soon become clear that the unrelenting priority of most dishes is beef, lamb, chicken, rabbit, fish, or quail. The test of a chef's depth and breadth of skills is rarely how they cook fiddleheads or asparagus; generally, it's how they handle a rarer cut that requires technique and knowledge to prepare properly. Sometimes it's something like cheek or tongue, which many North Americans treat as an off-cut— and you could argue that these shows, in demonstrating what is possible, are encouraging us to take a more holistic approach to eating animals, one more in line with developing a relationship with a butcher rather than getting chicken breasts on sale at Loblaws and further enriching Galen Weston Jr. What is simultaneously true, though, is the focus remains on meat. If a contestant on *Chopped* burns their asparagus tips, it's not great, but they may still get through; if they overcook their fillet or neglect to remove the tough outer layer of skin from beef tongue, they may as well remove and fold their apron on the spot. Flair with vegetables is treated as an asset, not a core requirement.

In Jeffrey Steingarten's essay "Where's the *Boeuf*?" he writes that steamed broccoli is "the root of all evil." But he also writes approvingly about visiting Alain Passard's Arpège, which was one of only twenty-one restaurants in France in the early 2000s with a three-star Michelin rating, and which had recently shifted its main focus from animal-based foods to plant-based foods. Steingarten describes his meal at Arpège as "stunning, original, precise, provocative, and very delicious."

It's true that growing beans, pulses, grains, and vegetables, in general, creates a much smaller ecological footprint than growing meat; it's true that industrial-scale livestock practices generally do not respect animals. It's also true that dishes centred on beans and pulses and grains and vegetables can be satisfying, and hearty, and flavourful. I don't think the Food Network should suddenly become meat-free; I do think that if you approach non-meat as an afterthought, that approach will become self-propagating. If *Chopped* required the same care of leeks as it did of cow's tongue, it would make for more imaginative viewing, a different kind of cooking inspiration.

Even Anthony Bourdain changed his tune after visiting India for *Parts Unknown*. "I am dismissive and sometimes contemptuous of food that is made with a narrow world view as its first priority," he told *Vogue India* in 2017. "This is not the case in India, one of the few places on earth, where eating vegetarian is not a burden. In Punjab, wildly varying textures, huge selections, thrilling blends of spices and assertive, delicious flavours are always accompanied by wonderful, freshly made breads."

Today, rather than working, I'd like to be baking a cake. There's half a cup of reduced raspberry purée in my freezer, alongside some egg whites left over from making custard for ice cream. I am envisioning a two-layer raspberry white cake iced with chocolate Swiss meringue buttercream—maybe a two-day project, because my favourite way to bake is unhurriedly, while listening to an audiobook.

This kind of food-envisioning is pleasurable to me. When I was sick—eventually I was diagnosed with a type of chronic gastritis that is "strongly associated" with celiac disease—my thoughts regularly gravitated to what I might eat next, or soon, in a way that felt desperate. In retrospect, my body was hounding me. Some mornings or afternoons, working the communications job I had at the time, I'd find myself daydreaming, unaware of when exactly my mind had drifted away from faulty parallelism towards when I might next have a rice wafer with smoked salmon.

If you snapped a photo of me right now, placed it next to a photo from when I was ill, and took an Ipsos poll of Canadians asking them which was the "after," the majority would probably choose the thinner me, the unwell me, because that's how we've been inculcated to think about health.

But I am healthier now. I'm stronger, only rarely feel sick after I eat, and my appetite is back to what feels normal for me. I'm more well mentally too. Thinking about food is like a pleasantly sunny day with a breeze, rather than a punishingly humid one during a heat dome. When I describe myself as happily plump, I mean it.

As my body healed and I gained weight and I was able to digest a wider variety of foods, my reliance on almond milk and chia seeds and sunflower butter lessened, and I turned back to cow's milk and peanut butter. Though I'd made a choice to eat meat, it remained rarer in my diet than beans and eggs and tofu. Per-capita meat consumption in the U.S. comes in at around 225 pounds per year, while I consume under ten—other than a brief period while I was pregnant, anemic, and regularly purchasing off-cuts of beef from the butcher at Jean-Talon Market in Montreal.

It will always be odd to me that cooks like Anthony Bourdain think this means I've rejected of "the pure enjoyment of food." Instead, it feels like I've worked double time to retain the joys of gluttony. I have to avoid gluten in order to remain well, so I've learned to bake and cook without it. I don't eschew meat to eschew pleasure; pleasure is readily available elsewhere.

two bags of lettuce

After work on a Wednesday, Will and I coax Sinclair into a blue polka-dot fleece and boots and head downtown. It's spring warm and sunny, a cornflower-blue sky. We walk to Coastal Cookery, a local restaurant with a view of the Algerine Passage between Texada and Ahgykson Islands. The ocean is calm for this time of year—small waves, some with gentle whitecaps.

Sinclair orders fish and chips and orange juice off the kid's menu; Will, chicken and waffles and a beer. I usually get the ribs, which are fall-apart tender and come with mashed potatoes and seasonal greens, but it feels more like a salad day. I get the backwoods greens and a Diet Coke.

Our friend Clare is working, and we're chatting when a runner brings out our food. My salad is stacked high on an oblong plate, a feast's worth, the absolute pile of vegetation my body has been craving.

When I eat this salad in March, executive chef Sean Hansen tells me, the restaurant sources its lettuce mix through the food distributor Sysco, which taps into the global supply chain to keep shelves and walk-ins stocked with produce, seafood, meat and poultry, dairy, and pantry staples year-round. To serve the west coast of Canada, in the late fall and winter, this lettuce is grown in Yuma, Arizona—one of the sunniest places in the world and the "winter lettuce capital of America," according to Antonio De Loera-Brust, communications director for United Farm Workers—and in arid spots of Southern California, such as the Imperial Valley.

From June until October, the lettuce in this salad will come from Terra Nostra ("Our land," in Italian), a farm located a ten-minute drive, or half-hour bike ride, down the road. It's the farm where my friend Jen works alongside four or five or six other farmhands; Will and I have gotten a community-supported agriculture (CSA) box from Terra Nostra for the past few years.

Much of the reporting and writing done about more ecologically friendly and equitable food has focused on small-scale local food with a sustainability focus, and I understand why: it uses less fossil fuel to ship, farmers are more able to focus on soil health, and we are more easily able to influence things on the local political level. If we want to see better labour conditions, or more stringent animal welfare rules, or are concerned about runoff in a local creek, it's theoretically easier to lobby, harangue, or gently encourage our neighbours.

Moreover, as J.B. MacKinnon, co-author of *The 100-Mile Diet*, points out on a phone call, change is possible through consumer pressure on food systems in a way that isn't quite as possible in other areas of our lives—because we eat about three times a day and spend so much of our money on what we eat.

"The thing that ended up really actually blowing my mind about that experience was how dramatic an impact the local food movement had on the landscape," he tells me, reflecting on what it was like to try out the hundred-mile experiment just as the local eating movement took off.

"It changed the way people were actually doing things and changed what people were growing in different areas in a way that was highly visible," he says. "We did see a whole bunch of system-level changes, none of them revolutionary, but all of them, and especially all of them together, adding up to something pretty impressive."

Small-scale farmers in the province have made great strides, but the reality is that the majority of what sustains most of us in the winter in Canada comes from elsewhere. In B.C., it is often California that is feeding us—a state that's facing intense drought pressures on top of the usual caveats about conventional large-scale agriculture, such as the fact that oil and gas are running out, we're facing fertilizer shortages, and agricultural greenhouse gas emissions in the U.S. and Canada account for about 11 percent and 10 percent of our annual output, respectively (not including emissions from fossil fuel usage or fertilizer production). The labour conditions on large conventional farms are also often abominable: labourers are frequently illegally paid piece rates that don't add up to minimum wage, and agricultural employers are regularly cited for not following legally mandated rest breaks and for wage theft.

For a long time, for anyone who's been paying attention, it has felt like industrial food systems have been borrowing from the future—including labourers' futures—and the necessarily heavy consequences are looming.

Considering my heaping mound of greens, two sets of questions emerge. First: on a systems level, if we wanted to eat locally and sustainably year-round, what could that look like? Is it possible?

And second: if for the near future, the majority of what we eat will continue to come through the global supply chain via conventional agriculture, what could, or should, we be doing to extend our sphere of influence to the places where our food is grown and harvested? Are conventional agriculture's sustainability and labour practices reformable in any meaningful way?

In early winter, when the sun is rising at 8:16 a.m. in Powell River, it's up at 6:42 about 2,500 kilometres south in the Imperial Valley. The valley is tucked into the very southeastern part of California, near the Mexican border to the south and the Arizonan border to the east. It would be desert dry if not for land speculators building a canal westward from the Colorado River in 1901. (It was a failure of this canal that created the now heavily polluted Salton Sea in 1905.) A new canal, the All-American Canal, was constructed in the 1930s as part of the New Deal and began delivering water to Imperial Valley in 1940. This canal runs eighty miles (about 128 kilometres) from the Colorado in the east to the Imperial Valley in the west, relies on gravity, and has been the sole source of water to the area since 1942.

Water drawn from the Colorado River has enabled farmers in the Imperial Valley to grow lush green crops like lettuce that otherwise wouldn't grow well, if at all, in this climate. But drought and overreliance on the Colorado, which starts in the Rocky Mountains and runs southwest to the Gulf of California in Mexico, supplying irrigation and drinking water along the way, mean it's drying up. Farmers in the Imperial Valley draw more water from the Colorado than the states of Arizona and Nevada together—and their senior water rights mean they're legally entitled to do so. But as the river begins to disappear, even these farmers are facing cutbacks; they need to give up 10 percent of their supply.

The lettuce grown for the salad I'm eating in March was most likely sown in late October or early November. It likes the sandy, loamy soil of the desert. It was either sown as pelleted seed—a seed encapsulated in clay, which makes it easier to handle—using a machine called a precision planter, or it was transplanted as seedlings in paper pots or little cubes of soil, using a different kind of machine. Both machines move effectively to cover a large terrain, which is helpful since the average farm in California is about 351 acres. This translates into the Vatican City three times over, or about 266 football fields. If you stand at the end of the row, it's lettuce, lettuce, lettuce as far as the eye can see.

After seeding, the lettuces are usually watered by sprinklers for the first five to seven days, until the seeds germinate and the seedlings emerge. Farmers then switch to furrow irrigation; the soil is depressed between the lettuce rows and then those paths, or furrows, are flooded, watering the lettuce from the bottom and the side. In this arid environment, it usually takes about three acre-feet, or 3,700 cubic metres, of water per acre to grow leaf lettuce. To conserve water, some farmers are switching to drip line irrigation. (But something called the paradox of irrigation efficiency can mean switches like these don't equal more water left in the watershed; farmers often use the savings to increase their irrigated crop area or grow more water-intensive produce.)

The soil is helped along by fertilization—as much as 250 pounds per acre of phosphorus pre-planting and between 200 and 250 pounds per acre of nitrogen via side-dressing when the lettuces have begun to grow. Conventional herbicides are sprayed to help control weeds; conventional pesticides are sprayed to help control insects, such as aphids, leaf miners, and the silverleaf whitefly.

The lettuce destined for my salad grows slowly but surely through the winter and is ready to pick by early March, let's say March 1. It's chilly in the morning, about 9 degrees Celsius, and cloudy. By noon, it will hit a high of 17.

The harvest itself is a carefully orchestrated agricultural ballet. I've never seen it in person, but it's a whole niche genre on YouTube.

A farm worker who goes by Chore Vlogs, for example, films a March day in his life working for Andrew Smith Company in Greenfield, California: he picks out a ball cap, makes some coffee to keep warm, catches a company bus to the field. "The landscape is beautiful," he says in Spanish, arriving at the farm and training his camera in a slow circle, capturing the mountains ringing the fields. When it's time to pick, about a dozen farm workers form mini production lines, bending, beheading the lettuce, and knocking off a few outer leaves before tucking it into clear plastic bags affixed to a belt around their waists and placing it on the outstretched metal arms of a machine that is slowly inching across the field. Packers tape the bags closed and place the lettuces into black plastic crates and cardboard boxes and onto a conveyer belt, which runs down the centre of the machine, towards a truck that quickly fills with full crates and boxes.

"The speed of those guys is impressive," says another man, David T., who films field workers in the United States. David T., speaking in Spanish, pans the vast field. "We walk for hours, friends," he says.

The social media feeds of United Farm Workers also offer a peek behind the scenes and a bit of education about what farm life is like—heat, flooding, rain, snow. "My work is very hard," a lettuce loader named Ismael tells UFW. "We work in different climates, cold, heat, and rain. Thanks to farm workers, the country has food. We deserve to be treated as people, not just tools in the fields."

After it's harvested, the lettuce must be kept cold—at a temperature right above freezing—and in humid conditions, it will keep well for two or three weeks.

The path from the field in Imperial Valley, California, to Coastal Cookery probably consists of initial cold storage at or near the farm; the lettuce then travels by refrigerated truck or rail, making its way to Sysco's Victoria, B.C., distribution centre before being trucked up to Powell River.

Sysco is one of, if not *the*, largest food distributor in the world. But it feels a bit like a black box. I know that it serves Coastal Cookery, and I know it serves other restaurants in the area too. Its big refrigerated eighteen-wheelers park outside any given establishment making deliveries, the back door open, ramp down.

The first time I try to reach the distribution centre that services Powell River, it's April 2022. I ask for three things: to visit the facility, to interview someone who can chat a bit about the produce sources for this facility, and to go on a ride-along from Victoria to Powell River with a delivery driver. When I finally manage to make contact with someone on the phone, she says she'll get back in touch soon to see if she can make arrangements. When I ask for a callback number, she says the main line will do. But no one ever answers the main line again, and the phone system is labyrinthine. I send follow-up emails every once in a while for a year before I give up.

In Canada, Sysco has thirty cold and dry storage facilities spanning 4,150,000 square feet, or about ninety-five acres. The company earned more than $68 billion in fiscal year 2022, growing annual sales by 36.9 percent and returning $1.5 billion to shareholders. "We could not have accomplished these impressive results without the more than 71,000 associates at Sysco, whose passion and dedication fuel our success," president and CEO Kevin Hourican wrote in a letter to stockholders, opening the 2022 annual report.

Reviews from drivers on Indeed—numbering over five thousand—are middling, often mentioning the physicality of the job. ("Twenty thousand pounds or say eight hundred boxes to deliver, probably to seventeen locations in one shift," reads one. "Insane. If you are between twenty-five to thirty years old you can do the job ... Older ones don't even think about it.")

By the end of March 2023, over a thousand drivers and warehouse workers have gone on strike against the company in

Indiana, Kentucky, and California, alleging excessive overtime and demanding higher wages and better health care benefits. "We regret the union has chosen to walk out on our customers instead of working in good faith to reach an agreement at the table," Sysco says in a press release about the strike in Indianapolis. "Sysco Indianapolis has implemented its contingency plans to quickly ramp up operations to serve our customers despite the Teamsters leadership's actions to disrupt deliveries to hospitals, nursing homes, schools and local small businesses. Sysco Indianapolis has also filed an unfair labour practice charge with the National Labor Relations Board contesting Local 135's bad faith bargaining actions."

A few thousand kilometres away from the striking workers, and a bit earlier in the season, I'm at Blueberry Commons, where I used to volunteer, asking lead farmer Ron Berezan my twin questions: Could we farm locally at scale, and if so, how? And if conventional agriculture is going to continue to constitute the majority of what feeds us, can we reform it?

"Is it reformable?" Ron echoes my question back to me, rolling it around for consideration. "I think that from the very beginning, it was predicated on a misunderstanding of mathematics. In other words, that you can keep subtracting and never add, and somehow continue to produce—it's extractive by definition."

Ron is referring to soil health when he describes conventional agriculture as extractive—to grow a crop, it takes nutrients, mines soil fertility, and adds back selectively, rather than holistically, to regenerate fertility. In another conversation, with farmer Aaron Mazurek, who owns Terra Nostra, he goes so far as to set the term "conventional" aside. Conventional, he says, should be what we call the kind of farming people have done for hundreds and thousands of years. What we currently call conventional—so we can distinguish it from organic—should more rightly be called *chemical* agriculture. "I prefer chemical agriculture, because that's really what it is. It's based on fossil fuels and chemicals," he says.

Conventional ag is not just extractive when it comes to soil fertility—it also often relies on an extractive approach to labour that does not adequately compensate people for their hard work and considerable skills. Migrant workers, who make up a large proportion of agricultural workers in Canada and the U.S., are often dependent on their employers for their visas and fear retaliation if they speak up about health and safety violations.

Where ecological offences and labour offences intersect, the results can be sad, even gruesome: a recent paper put together for the UC Merced Community and Labor Center Farmworker Health Study found that for farm workers, chronic exposure to pesticides can cause adverse birth effects, cancer in children, genotoxicity, declined neuropsychological functioning, cancer, and cardiovascular diseases in adults.

Posts from the UFW always carry a hashtag: #WeFeedYou. It can be hard, especially considering the recent pace of inflation and how expensive groceries are right now, to factor in the costs associated with this kind of agriculture that we don't pay at the till—the costs to labourers, and the costs to the land and water where these labourers live. But they form part of what goes into each and every bag of conventionally grown lettuce that comes to B.C. from California in the winter months and much of what is produced conventionally right here in the province.

On a weekday in early spring, the first week the farmers at Terra Nostra are back at it for the season, Jen and I stop for coffee at my favourite local coffee shop and head south in her Subaru. It's a quick drive to the farm and we've lucked out—it's not raining. We turn left off the highway and head east a short ways until we reach a red outbuilding with metal siding. To the right, there are a few tiny homes. To the left, the fields are blanketed in a light dusting of cover crops, and a bit farther, a ridge, or hill, with a yurt nestled in amongst some trees. (Every small coastal farm in B.C., from my experience, holds about a 33 percent chance of yurt.)

Jen lets us into the building. A whiteboard outlines farm chores; they're from the end of last season, Jen says—they haven't quite flipped things over yet for the year. A card tacked to the whiteboard reads, "Farm to Table and Table to Soul."

Soon, Aaron Mazurek arrives. They're behind schedule this year because of the cold snap, he says while giving me a tour. They've prepped and seeded some of the soil in the 32-by-165-foot greenhouse—with spinach, spring mix, radishes, salad turnips, beets, and carrots—and have started some alliums, but will be catching up today on lettuces and brassicas.

This is the farm's eighth season, and by now they've got their schedule "pretty dialled in," Aaron says. The plant varieties they're growing—over a hundred on about three acres—are organized by field and planting date, colour-coded in a white binder.

I help Jen seed lettuce in 128-cell trays. We add soil, compress it a bit, and place a rectangular wooden block fitted with 128 small dowels, upside down, which creates a divot in the centre of each cell. Next we place a pelleted seed into the divot. When the tray is full of seeds, we add more potting mix on top, compress again, and wipe off the excess. We then carry the trays over to flood tables, also known as ebb and flow tables; each of these holds fourteen trays, and they fill and drain from the bottom, rather than overhead. This waters the seedlings more efficiently and helps prevent damping off—the disappointing death of baby seedlings following their initial eruption from the soil. In about three weeks or a month, when the seedlings are strong, they'll be transplanted outdoors, where they'll be watered using buried drip line. The water feeding Terra Nostra's farm comes mostly from a drilled well.

The greens we're starting today will crop in about seventy-five days. The lettuce destined for Coastal Cookery is an organic analogue of Salanova, productive in a number of sub-varieties for salad mix. The pelletized seeds look like little forbidden Cadbury Mini Eggs in my palm. Terra Nostra will grow green and red leaf lettuce and some other varieties to add flavour and texture. These lettuces are one of their top sellers; they'll seed weekly to keep up with demand. About 1,600 lettuce plants fit into each of Terra Nostra's two-hundred-foot rows.

Aaron walks me through the harvest process. The farmers will head out into the field first thing in the morning—the cool start of the day will find the lettuce at its freshest and tastiest. (Picked in the heat and direct sun of the afternoon, it is grumpy and bitter.) Aaron grabs a bread knife and mimics the act of harvesting; they'll cut an inch or two above the ground, peeling off a few outer leaves, and the lettuce will regenerate, allowing them to get two or maybe even three harvests from each plant before replacing them with a new hardened-off seedling. Once it's cut, it goes into a big blue Rubbermaid bin and then into the walk-in cooler, which is kept at 2 or 3 degrees. Each Rubbermaid holds about twenty pounds of lettuce, and they'll fill three or four bins per harvest, totalling sixty or eighty pounds.

After it's harvested, it goes into the bubbler—a big metal trough that has a Hudson valve, which switches off the water when the tub is full, so whoever is harvesting can busy themselves with other things. Two pipes in the bottom of the greens washer are connected to a jacuzzi pump, and they agitate the greens gently to remove dirt. Next, bright orange tubs that look like laundry baskets are used to scoop the greens up and move them over to a commercial salad spinner. The goal at this point is to get the lettuce as dry as possible, Aaron says. If it's wet in the bag, it will rot.

Then the lettuce goes into a blue tote and finally gets weighed and bagged. Last year, Aaron says, they sent about five pounds of lettuce a week to a local roaster and coffee shop. Coastal Cookery got about six pounds twice a week. Much of the lettuce is bagged at about a half-pound per bag and goes to CSA deliveries, a local small butcher shop, and the farm store. The deliveries are done by farm workers; when I'm introduced to Graeme, he knows what my backyard garden looks like, because he's been dropping off blue totes on my driveway for the past few years.

Terra Nostra is certified organic, which means they're required to follow a variety of rules and regulations about soil amendments and fertilizers, pesticides, herbicides, veterinary drugs, food additives, and animal welfare. They employ about a half-dozen local full-time and part-time workers for the season. They try to pay above minimum wage, Aaron tells me, and two of their employees bought homes while working at the farm. Workers at Terra Nostra also take home vegetables from the farm, feeding themselves with what they grow.

Graeme lives in the yurt and raises chicken, turkeys, and pigs to sell. Their manure is used to add fertility to the soil—it's not quite enough, Aaron says, and they have to bring in compost from elsewhere, but it helps. They test the soil annually and amend it if it's deficient in certain micronutrients, such as boron. They weed by hand and for pest control, use netting to keep out insects like cabbage worms, aphids, and the carrot rust fly. About 5 percent of the lettuce crop will be lost to wireworm, Aaron says, but he's not too worried about it.

Back-of-the-napkin math, Aaron calculates it would take about a hundred farms the size of Terra Nostra to feed the fourteen thousand or so people who live in our area. And that's just for vegetables—we'd also need to sort out grains and pulses, meat, and dairy. Things like coffee and chocolate, which few of us are willing to give up, will always need to come from elsewhere.

While an eating-local-at-scale scenario probably means that we would (societally) need to eat far less meat and dairy than we currently do, cutting it out entirely isn't feasible or, in the long term, desirable. Meat and dairy are high-calorie foods that are important in the winter months in cold climates, and the manure from animal agriculture, like that from the pigs and turkeys and chickens being raised by Graeme at Terra Nostra, is an important source of soil fertility.

In the winter, they could potentially use the greenhouse—in our zone, cooler-weather crops will grow in unheated greenhouses—but the plants would grow much more slowly, as we're almost at the fiftieth parallel here, and on our darkest winter days, we only get about eight hours of sun.

"Light is the limiting factor," Aaron says.

Of course, eating local (or farm to table) isn't always a synonym for sustainable or ethical or labour-friendly. One of the most cited exemplars of the form used to be Dan Barber, the chef and owner of Blue Hill at Stone Barns; the concept of his restaurant is a menuless prix fixe where the day's dishes are determined by what's harvested on-site. But a three-part exposé published by *Eater* in 2022 detailed an environment "rife with grinding pressure and explosions of anger." This wasn't the first time Blue Hill at Stone Barns had come under fire; five years earlier, in 2017, the company settled a two-million-dollar class-action wage theft lawsuit.

And Blue Hill is not alone; in 2021, the *New York Times* ran an exposé on Willows Inn, located on Lummi Island in the Pacific Northwest, alleging a "toxic," "abusive" workplace that included physical and verbal intimidation, slurs, and sexual harassment.

"There's no such thing as ethical food," a farm worker told me a few years ago, near the end of the growing season. "More ethical?" I asked, referring to our local context. He shrugged, conceding.

"There certainly is a tendency to think that small farm, local farm, organic farm, all equal good farms," says Antonio De Loera-Brust, communications director for the United Farm Workers. "And maybe those things are good for other reasons. But there's no correlation with, you know, being small, local, organic [and] necessarily treating your workers right. You can be doing all that stuff, and that does not in and of itself mean that you're going to treat workers with the dignity that they deserve."

One of the most "stunning" farming statistics is that a high percentage of farm labourers struggle with food insecurity, De Loera-Brust says. "The very workers who are feeding us often struggle to put food on the table for their own families."

The solution, he says, is for workers to unionize. California is only one of two states in the U.S. where agriculture workers have the legal right to unionize. (The other state is New York.)

De Loera-Brust also recommends that consumers focus on buying food from unionized farms. Co-op and independent grocers focused on organics or sustainability can opt to make this part of their purchasing strategy. Though it's trickier, consumers can do it themselves by checking the labels or fruit stickers for the farm name, De Loera-Brust says, and by writing to the grocery chain to note their preference for union-grown food.

Another consumer mindset shift might involve opting to eat seasonally, including consuming fewer fresh greens in the winter.

In Canada, this means we'd eat things like salad from May to October, eschewing them for stored root vegetables and pickled, frozen, and dried vegetables from November to April, with the addition, at least on the West Coast, of cold-hardy vegetables with long harvest windows, such as kale, Brussels sprouts, and cabbages.

At Coastal Cookery, owner Sarah McClean and executive chef Sean Hansen tell me they prioritize labour, sustainability, and local growing in their decision-making processes. But, McClean says, the restaurant can't be recreating its menu every day to suit what's come in from local growers—they need regular dishes each cook can learn to create consistently, alongside specials they can feature for a reasonable duration, maybe a month's time, in the summer.

What changed things for Coastal Cookery, McClean and Hansen agree, was the establishment of a few local farms, such as Terra Nostra, that have an understanding of their needs as a restaurant and that can consistently deliver reasonable amounts of certain kinds of produce, like the lettuce mix that ends up on my plate.

When I ask McClean and Hansen why purchasing from local growers is important to them, both pause. They're also participating in a composting program that diverts much of what would end up in the landfill to a local facility, McClean says. They make their sauces in-house. Put care into their food. It's just baked into their values to support local agriculture. It costs more to do so, but it's a worthwhile investment in community and sustainability.

McClean also says that the growth of local small-scale agriculture, and consumer desire for that agriculture, has spurred important changes in the ways companies like Sysco and its competitors operate.

"Similar to craft beer, and what pressure that put on Molson Canadian to adapt their business model," McClean says, Sysco has begun to recognize that small farms do have good produce, but they need support. "Sysco's done a lot of work with local farms, smaller farms, almost brokering for them in the sense of giving them the capacity to expand their growth so that they can be sustainable for a wholesale market," she says. "Because also for a lot of farmers, it's not a nice life to go and slog at the market for two days, three days a week, and just try and get rid of everything."

But homes and restaurants are just two of the places people eat; some of the systems-wide solutions are easier to seek for institutions like universities and hospitals, which purchase and cook at larger quantities with regularized meals and more predictable demand.

Hayley Lapalme and Jennifer Reynolds, executive directors of Nourish, work with hospitals to reform their food offerings to better meet patients' cultural needs, bring dignity back into kitchens for workers, and build and support local sustainable food systems.

There is often dissonance for hospitals, they say over a Zoom call, in the way budgets reflect food values. "It's treated like parking," Lapalme says. In other words, just another budget item, rather than one of the building blocks of patient health.

CHU Sainte-Justine in Montreal—incidentally, the hospital where I gave birth to Sinclair via C-section, meaning we were there for a few days—managed to shift its food offerings in a way that saw an increase in patient satisfaction from 50 percent to 99 percent, and a decrease in food waste from 45 percent to 5 percent. Patients are now eating way more of the food they're served, nourishing their bodies and supporting healing. Fifty percent of CHU Sainte-Justine's menu is now vegetarian or vegan, 64 percent of what they source is local, and 6 percent is organic.

Hospitals can use their big purchasing power, Lalalme and Reynolds say, to effect big changes in procurement and the supply chain, matching supply up with demand. And for CHU Sainte-Justine, after an initial capital investment, the conversion to this approach to feeding their patients was net neutral for their budget.

What's harder for an individual person or family to do at a grocery store chain, in other words, is easier for institutions to do at scale.

So change is possible. But it's tricky. Lettuce, for example, can be grown as a greenhouse crop year-round but requires additional light (and sometimes heat) in the winter, which can be a costly energy draw. In some areas of the country—including Windsor-Essex, prime Ontario growing land, where electricity demand is expected to double over the next five years—greenhouses are the largest driver of increased demand for electricity.

One new B.C. business, based in Pitt Meadows, recently told the CBC that it could produce "up to six million bags of salad greens" per year—baby leafy greens, grown vertically, using grow lights. The vertical farm, according to one of its owners, "uses 99 percent less agricultural land, 99 percent less freshwater, and 99 percent less fertilizer than traditional farming practices." But the article leaves out electricity use—a key factor when growing vertically and indoors. If part of the goal of local agriculture is to cut down on energy expenditures in shipping, indoor farming does not present a very viable solution.

Aaron from Terra Nostra suggests a different, much simpler, if more labour-intensive solution. There's a great book called *Farmers of Forty Centuries*, he tells me, written by Franklin Hiram

King, who toured China, Korea, and Japan in 1909—before commercial fertilizers were available. These intensive systems, Aaron says, recycled all of the human and animal manure, all of the vegetable waste, and it went back into the system, and the systems fed millions of people. On the municipal level, this is an involved but available fix: organic waste can be composted and reused to support soil fertility instead of being sent to the landfill, where it does nothing but create methane.

"All agriculture was sustainable a hundred years ago, because we had no chemical fertilizer," he says. "It's not that we can't do it. It's already been done. We could do it today. It's just a mindset. It's cultural."

So we could reuse waste, but we could also reduce it and focus on getting more of what we produce on tables. A 2021 paper in the journal *Resources, Conservation & Recycling* found that about 14 percent of food is "lost before it even reaches the retail level." Suggested solutions included shifting away from the model of offering tax incentives for donations, which farmers often find too time-consuming and difficult to take advantage of, and shifting towards investing in processing infrastructure, which allows farmers to turn "ugly" produce into value-added foods; hooking farmers up with alternative markets such as farm-to-school programs; and focusing on price support and stabilization for produce.

Further waste happens at the retail and consumer levels. In B.C., the government estimates that organic waste represents about 40 percent of the material sent to landfills. Not all of this will be edible or directly recoupable, of course—some of it consists of things like eggshells and the tough outer leaves of cabbages and the half-eaten peanut butter sandwiches that come home in a five-year-old's lunch box. In the case of retail-level waste, some can be diverted or avoided by matching businesses with programs they can donate to. Consumer-level waste can be reduced by shifting to meal-planning and by learning how to process to freeze, dry, or can on-the-cusp vegetables before they turn. These practices require social support, though—via in-school food literacy and farm-to-school programs and by people making living wages or receiving enough social or disability income to have the time and mental space to lessen food waste.

These incremental steps would help us make the shift to more sustainable agriculture. Supporting unionized labour at home and abroad, as De Loera-Brust suggests, would have immediate material benefits for farm workers—and potential secondary benefits, if farms are forced, via government legislation, to retool their approaches to chemical use to protect labourers. And supporting local agriculture would help us build strong local food systems—in the way that Coastal Cookery and Nourish do, and by buying directly from farmers and through programs like CSA boxes. Nothing would change overnight, but it would change eventually.

Back at Coastal Cookery, I tuck into my salad, which is composed of slightly bitter crunchy greens, refreshingly tart pickled golden beets, lightly candied walnuts, crispy bacon, and thin slices of apple and red onion, all dressed in a simple vinaigrette.

The salad is good, and I'm grateful for it and all the labour that went into it. It can be easy, I think, to feel a sense of alienation from this labour when purchasing produce from a restaurant or grocery store, when there are more, and longer, links in the supply chain. I feel like the salad mix I helped seed is more special because of all the relationships and connections I have to it. But though the trip is longer for the Californian lettuce, it's still a trip from farm to table. The greens are still growing in soil, watered by rain and rivers and aquifers, powered by the warmth of the sun, picked by skilled labourers, just like my friends here, who deserve good working conditions and living wages. I think that part of the mystery of multinational corporations, their focus on perfect produce available consistently, is designed to obfuscate the particular origins of that produce as a material good that has been grown and harvested and packed and shipped by workers we would otherwise be in solidarity with.

And part of our responsibility as people nourishing ourselves is to recognize this labour, familiarize ourselves with it if it's not part of our everyday life, and contribute to meaningful structural change in whatever ways we can, both locally and through solidarity with the people growing, harvesting, and processing our food in places we're connected to primarily through vast complex supply chains. The system we have in place now is unsustainable, a miracle and a mess. But reforming it can be empowering, can build community, can help us feel like we are participating, rather than extracting; participating, rather than being extracted from. Feeding ourselves while building and sustaining so much more than just ourselves.

tomato chutney, part I:
reviving my nana's recipe

A few Septembers ago, I harvested two green bell peppers and a bunch of celery—twisting it at the base so that its leftover roots could feed the soil. I gathered Roma tomatoes and Gala apples I'd previously picked from my garden, and red peppers and onions from the grocery store, and I made my nana's tomato chutney for the first time, ever, by myself.

My nana was then in her nineties and living in a retirement home in small-town Ontario, having recently sold the well-kept split-level house in Burlington where my brother and I spent our summers with her and my granddad. My childhood home was chaotic; my parents fought, my mother drank, our bills were overdue. I was plump and my mother helped me diet, starting at the age of eight. (In the '90s, this meant caramel-flavoured rice cakes, butter-popcorn-flavoured rice cakes, apple-cinnamon-flavoured rice cakes.) My internal goal for each day was to eat eight hundred calories or less. I rarely felt at ease.

At my grandparents' house, my granddad gardened and made compost. His garden stretched over the bottom of the backyard, with his compost bin in the corner. He showed my brother and me how to rewire a lamp. We did the crossword together. He taught me all the math he'd learned at the night classes he'd taken after immigrating to Canada. He wrote stories about his time in the war and as a young electrician first on a typewriter and then on a computer in the basement. My nana taught us how to play a card game called clock solitaire, gave us old hardcover Nancy Drews to read in the sunroom, and turned the produce my granddad harvested into lunch and dinner and preserves.

My grandparents' calm, unwavering attention made me feel secure and loved—and my nana's attention often crystallized in the form of eight-ounce jars of chutney, made and set aside especially for me. My favourite way to eat it was on cheese-and-chutney sandwiches, cut on a diagonal, the sweet, tart, slightly crunchy red chutney contrasting with crumbly, pungent cheddar.

When I was entering my mid-twenties, the prostate cancer my granddad had lived with and undergone treatment for since I was a child finally spread. I'd moved out of my parents' house by then and was living about forty-five kilometres north of my grandparents. My mother and stepfather gave me one of their old cars, a lozenge-shaped blue Taurus, and I drove from Guelph to Burlington once a week to stay over with my grandparents, leaving early in the morning to get back to my new communications job.

When I was twenty-six, after my granddad had died and I'd moved across the country to go back to school, my mother disowned me. She'd stumbled across an essay I'd written about our strained relationship, one I hadn't meant for her to see.

My relationships with the rest of my maternal family also became more tense, more sad. It was supposed to stay a secret, what I had written about. I was supposed to feel gutted when she disowned me. I was supposed to apologize.

At thirty-three, when I gave birth to Sinclair, my nana didn't answer my calls. I found out she didn't want to meet Sinclair unless I rekindled a relationship with my mother, whom I hadn't spoken to for years. Maybe she felt it would be a betrayal to meet my child if my mother most likely never would—but the silence felt like a betrayal to me too. Like my own belonging to the family was conditional and not as primary as my mother's. Like I would need to fend for myself again, the way I had as a child, fearing my mother's alcoholism and anger and her desire, above all, to keep up appearances. But this time without the respite of my grandparents' love and steady care.

My nana's chutney recipe calls for twenty-four ripe tomatoes, six apples, one bunch of celery, three medium onions, two green peppers, two red peppers, sugar, vinegar, salt, mustard seeds, cloves, and ginger. I skin the tomatoes after dunking them into boiling water, and chop everything into a fine dice. I place the tomatoes, onion, and celery in a colander overnight to drain any excess water. The next day, when everything is in the pot and begins to warm, the house fills with the chutney's smell, a smell that I haven't experienced in years. A smell I can now identify as the result of the recipe's unique combination of green pepper, tomatoes, and cloves.

The recipe I have is in my nana's hand. She wrote a letter to go alongside it, sent several years before the maternal side of my family stopped talking to me. When I wrote the first draft of this essay, I couldn't even remember where I was living when she sent it. Now, the memory has returned: I was living in a Guelph neighbourhood called the Ward with two bunnies named Acorn and Bigwig. I called her when the recipe arrived in the mail. We talked as I was doing the dishes, and I almost dropped my phone in the sink.

The recipe bears my name: "Andrea's favourite tomato chutney."

After the chutney has cooled, I spoon some onto a piece of cheddar. It is the taste of being in my grandparents' kitchen at lunchtime. It is the clock ticking, the radio turned down but still broadcasting the news. It is the precise feeling of being safe and loved. Sinclair tries it with cheese and crackers; she likes it, and I feel grateful to be able to share something of my nana with her.

Once, when I was nine, we visited my grandparents for Christmas in Florida. I remember getting into the car to go home and not being able to say goodbye because I was crying and didn't want to leave. That temporary parting contained the kernel of the larger parting that, even as a child, I understood was to come. I began to hoard time with them. My granddad died when he was eighty-seven; I cried for two weeks straight and then didn't cry again for nearly two years, as if the loss had evaporated a reservoir. But I always felt my nana would live into her nineties, that she'd be alive alongside me when I was thirty-five, maybe even forty. I never guessed I could lose her earlier, in another way.

As the distance between us grew, I craved her chutney more fiercely. I'd moved across the country three times since she'd sent me the recipe, and I thought I'd lost it. I couldn't exactly call her and ask her to send another copy. Before I found the recipe folded into the pages of an old book—looking for something entirely different I'd also misplaced—I thought I'd never taste it again.

Having made it again, I miss my nana more fiercely too. I wish I could call her and tell her that I didn't have all the right canning tools, so when I introduced my mason jars to the canning bath, it created a geyser of boiling water. But also that my chutney was a success: it tasted just like hers. That I grew much of the produce I used to make it, as my granddad had for her. That I love her, and that I am sorry, but I'm not sorry enough to accept my mother's abuse as a condition of belonging to the family. That it was her early love, in fact, that helped make me a strong enough person to say no.

ANDREA'S FAVOURITE TOMATO CHUTNEY, FROM NANA

A note on canning safety: While improvisation and substitution is generally welcome in cooking, it's important to stick to the ingredients and proportions in recipes that are jarred and preserved in a water bath, like this chutney. A pH of 4.6 or lower is required for safe water bath canning.

TOOLS

- six hot, sterilized 500-millilitre (pint-size) mason jars and fresh canning lids
- knife, cutting board, and peeler
- large cooking pot
- water bath canning pot, jar rack, and jar tongs
- cheesecloth

INGREDIENTS

- 24 tomatoes (I used San Marzano/Roma tomatoes)
- 6 apples, peeled and chopped (I used Gala apples)
- 5 medium white onions, chopped
- 1 bunch celery, chopped finely
- 2 green peppers, chopped
- 2 red peppers, chopped
- 2 cups white sugar
- 2 cups white vinegar

- 1 teaspoon each of cloves, ginger, cinnamon, turmeric, and dried mustard
- 4 tablespoons mixed pickling spice (tied up in a cheesecloth bundle)
- 2 teaspoons pickling salt

1. Cut an X into the bottom of the tomatoes and place them into boiling water for one minute to remove skins. Then chop them into small pieces and place them in a colander over a bowl to drain. Chop onions and celery into fine pieces and place in the same colander. Sprinkle salt over mixture. Place colander and bowl in the fridge to drain overnight.
2. The next day, remove the contents from fridge, and after pressing lightly to remove excess fluid, pour the contents of the colander into a large cooking pot.
3. Chop green and red peppers and apples into small pieces and add to pot.
4. Stir in the rest of the ingredients, and mix well.
5. Place pot over medium heat until it reaches a gentle boil. Keep stirring until it is as thick as you want it— about two hours, the longer the thicker. You might have to lower the temperature to keep it at a gentle boil and not a full boil.
6. When done, remove the pickling spice bag.
7. While still hot, pour into sterilized jars, leaving half an inch of room at the top.
8. Can in a water bath.*

Good luck and enjoy. Love, Nana.

* My nana's recipe doesn't give specifics, but you can treat this like you're canning salsa. Put the lids onto the jars

and screw until finger tight. Then submerge the jars in a large pot of water, fitted with a canning rack, that has been brought to a rolling boil. Ensure the jars are covered fully, with an inch of water above the tops of the jars. Place the lid on the pot and keep it at a boil for thirty minutes, then use tongs to remove the jars and place them on a tea towel. I leave them on the counter until I'm sure they've sealed properly—generally overnight. Sealed properly, they'll keep in a cool, dark place for up to a year.

tomato chutney, part II:
the empire in a sandwich

"From food do all creatures come into being."
—*The Bhagavad Gita*

I n my nana's final year of life, she told my brother, who told me, that it would be okay to call her. So before she died in late 2020, at the age of ninety-five, I got to speak with her on the phone a couple final times. The conversations were short. She wanted to hear about Sinclair, and she wanted to know that I was happy. She didn't want to talk about herself. I told her I'd made her chutney, and there was a piece I'd written about it that I wanted her to read one day, when she was ready. The pandemic was less than a year old. I was worried about her—worried she'd get COVID, worried she'd be isolated. I wanted to visit, but I lived thousands of kilometres away, and it would have been irresponsible.

I first visited her grave in late 2021. My brother and I sludged through the swampy grass, our boots getting muddier, searching for where she'd been buried. When we got there, we weeded the small area in front of her gravestone, and I cried, and my brother and I hugged, and then we went home.

When I was growing up, I used to press my family members for information—details that would help me piece together the stories of their lives. My dad and my maternal grandfather and my paternal grandmother all shared freely, sometimes remembering something new as I jogged their memories with nosy follow-ups. But my nana often demurred. She told some stories—one about why she didn't like to put her head underwater while swimming—but kept much of what makes family stories fun, like scandals and fights and fissures and breakups and makeups, to herself. Though I regularly asked about it, she kept her birth year private until she reached her nineties; she preferred to share only fond memories of family members, such that much of what I learned about her family life was through what was left unspoken.

But it also came through in her habits, including her cooking and her food, which were the clearest connection with her past and one of the clearest demonstrations of her love and care. (When my grandfather developed high blood pressure and high cholesterol, for example, she switched from cooking with leftover bacon grease to cooking with lighter oils and making things like steamed fish.)

I never thought to ask my nana directly about the culture she was passing down in the form of food. Though I had the recipe for her chutney, I hadn't thought about where exactly it came from until my mid-thirties, and I never got the chance to ask her. While I was writing the essay about what chutney meant in our relationship, I began to wonder if someone had passed it down to her, or if it was something she'd picked up in her lifetime. Did she start making it when her kids were young? Or much later? Or maybe earlier, growing up in England?

I'm curious enough that I've been tempted to email my aunt, from whom I'm estranged, to ask. But this impulse to get to the heart of things is part of the reason we're estranged in the first place. So I opt not to, instead asking my father, who began attending family meals at my mother's house while he was in high school in the mid-1970s. His side of the family eats their cheese sandwiches and ploughman's lunches—bread, cheese, chutney, pickled onion—with Branston Pickle, a popular type of pickled chutney, first manufactured in 1922, that's often eaten in this application in England. (My nana was born just three years after Branston Pickle, in 1925.)

My dad says my nana's chutney was unique to him—he's never had another like it. But it was a staple of her household when he first entered it. This, and the recipe, are the two clues I have to go by.

There is a joke about the British—that they went a'colonizing in search of flavour and spice, only to then neglect, as a culture, to season their food.

In the sixteenth and seventeenth centuries, English cooks did tend to use spices, such as mace and cinnamon and nutmeg, to season their meats and meals. Herbs and spices were used for something like medicinal purposes in cooking, to "balance" the "humours."

Food historian Lizzie Collingham's *The Taste of Empire* traces (amongst many other things) the eventual decline of popularity of spices in savoury British cuisine. One chapter follows naval administrator and diarist Samuel Pepys and his wife on a mid-seventeenth-century excursion to a French restaurant, or "ordinary," which, Collingham writes, "rejected spice mixtures on the grounds that they disguised rather than enhanced flavour."

"As spices disappeared from English food, it became increasingly plain, dominated by roast and boiled meats, pastries and pies," Collingham writes. "These plain meat dishes were, however, always accompanied by pungent condiments: mustard, horseradish sauce, pickles or fruit jellies."

Over a video call, Collingham tells me that while British cuisine eventually relegated spices to the sweet course of the meal, flavourful condiments remained "really important." By the 1850s, she says, Indian curries made with curry powder had become quite fashionable, adorning middle-class dinner tables and being featured at parties. The middle classes also hashed cold meat with curry spices to make their leftovers more appealing.

This wouldn't quite have been my family: all the branches I'm familiar with were working class. I know less about my maternal ancestors, but my paternal ancestors worked in mills and as labourers and farmers and butchers. When Collingham asks, I tell her I know my nana came to Canada from England after the Second World War, as a nanny, and then worked in retail at the Bay; my grandfather enlisted in England at seventeen, hoping to become a pilot, but his eyesight was too poor. So he became an airplane mechanic instead. He came to Canada via the postwar red carpet that was rolled out for English veterans and began working as an electrician. Neither of my grandparents went past eighth grade in school.

While curries saw a rise in popularity in nineteenth-century Britain for the middle classes, as a direct result of the colonization of India—first Company Rule from 1773 to 1858, and then the British Raj until 1947—Brits didn't adopt the practice of eating chutneys, or relishes, with their curries. (They also simplified their cooking approaches and their spice blends, turning the wide variety of cuisines initially brought back from India into a much narrower spread of options that follow a similar cooking technique. But that's an essay lots of others have written.)

Chutneys and pickles, however, were "very, very much a working-class thing by the first half of the twentieth century," Collingham says. "Of all the Indian influences that might have got through to the British working classes, it tended to be piccalilli and Branston Pickle."

In the nineteenth century and earlier, the working classes, in particular farmers and farm labourers, or ploughmen, would have woken up, laboured for a few hours, and paused around eleven a.m. for sustenance, Collingham says. This meal would have consisted of a hunk of bread and often a raw onion and, if financially feasible, some cheese. Cheese was considered the labourer's "white meat"—the consumption of meat wasn't necessarily daily, perhaps confined to a Sunday roast. So the practice of eating chutney as part of this meal followed directly in the footsteps of eating meat with pungent condiments, and it was probably related to the practice of augmenting the meal with raw onion. When pickle became accessible to the working classes, it was added to the meal.

Peter Atkins, professor emeritus at Durham University with a specialization in the geographies of food and drink, traces a slightly different earlier cousin of the pickle in the ploughman's lunch. "I think it really began with anchovy sauce at the end of the nineteenth century in London," he says. "That was really, I think, the first and most popular addition to the British diet, based upon Italian anchovies." The beginning of the nineteenth century, Atkins says, marked the beginning of the various pickles. Their method of preservation relied on sugar—which had entered England much earlier, part of the triangular trade, with its own legacy of enslavement and colonialism—and vinegar. Unlike the vinegar on the continent, which was made using wine (hence vinegar, "vin aigre" or "sour wine"), Atkins says the

Brits used beer as the basis of their vinegar. Called malt vinegar, it most often relies on fermented barley and is still in use today.

In an article entitled "Vinegar and Sugar: The Early History of Factory-Made Jams, Pickles, and Sauces in Britain," Atkins traces the appearance of industrial-scale packaged goods preserved in sugar and vinegar in the late eighteenth and early nineteenth century, through companies like E. Lazenby & Son, Batty & Co., John Burgess and Son, and, notably, Crosse & Blackwell, which was one of the earliest, largest, and most successful manufacturers of pickles, table sauces, and other related products. In the mid-nineteenth century, Atkins writes, Crosse & Blackwell bypassed wholesale markets like the Covent Garden Market and purchased the produce they needed for their goods directly from farmers, whom they contracted. They also brewed their own vinegar—vertical integration. On our call, Atkins describes the company as "ruthless." The company grew throughout the early nineteenth century; by the 1860s, Atkins describes their output as "industrial" in scale. Crosse & Blackwell exported its goods to Australia, China, and India and advertised "extensively" in newspapers and magazines in Britain in the nineteenth century, reaching the middle classes and making the brand a household name. By the time the company began to manufacture Branston Pickle in 1922, it had honed its tactics; it used inexpensive, plentiful ingredients and advertised broadly to stir up familiarity and emotion—domestic bliss, nationalism, nostalgia.

When I ask him why he thinks Branston Pickle became so ubiquitous, Atkins confesses that he doesn't like it. "I think it's mainly the advertising," he says. "It was a very profitable product."

(After our interview, Atkins sends me the conference presentation his article was based on. It opens with a 1950 quote from an Italian man named Alberto Denti di Pirajno: "The British are ... 'incapable of giving any flavour to their food, [they] call on sauces to furnish to their dishes that which their dishes do not have. This explains the sauces, the jellies and prepared extracts, the bottled sauces, the chutneys, which populate the tables of this unfortunate people.'" He was a fascist during the Second World War, Atkins tells me. "So I'm not sure I believe anything he says, but I quoted it because it's a really nice indication of what other people think of the British diet.")

Echoing what Collingham told me, Atkin guesses pickles and chutneys wouldn't have been able to enter the working-class diet until after the working classes began to benefit from "improved purchasing ability" in the 1850s onwards, but markedly in the 1870s.

"They were being paid better wages," Atkins says. "And the food that they wanted to buy was falling relatively in price. The reason being—let's take bread for instance—because of the importation of wheat from Canada and America and various other places, with lower production costs in the Canadian prairies. It could be exported more cheaply. The flour was cheaper. And therefore the bread was cheaper."

Wheat became more economical to import after the demise of the Corn Laws (which had attempted to favour domestic agriculture by placing tariffs on staple grains like wheat and corn) in 1846. At first, it came mostly from the U.S.; by the late nineteenth and early twentieth century, it was coming mostly from Canada, which by 1910 was the world's largest wheat exporter.

Canada was able to achieve success in wheat exports because of the construction of the Canadian Pacific Railway, which allowed for relatively cheap transport of wheat across the country from the prairies. Both the railway and the "clearing" of the plains for agriculture were violent colonial undertakings.

In other words: every element of the ploughman's lunch—and my cheese and chutney sandwiches—are bound up in class, in history, in politics, in food systems, in empire. But this still doesn't quite answer where my nana's chutney came from.

There are hundreds of different kinds of regional chutneys and pickles eaten across India and South Asia. Some are sweet, some are spicy, some are cooling agents; some add interest and moisture to a meal heavier on rice or idli or dosa. Some are palate cleansers. Many were initially developed to use parts of plants, such as cauliflower leaves, that are nutritionally significant but require more treatment and attention to become delicious.

It could be tempting to dismiss the British approaches to chutney as pale comparisons of the originals. Or to say that British people are just eating chutneys wrong—or, perhaps, culturally appropriating them. If that's true, would it then be possible to decolonize a British chutney?

Simon Majumdar, a British-born cook, broadcaster, and author of Welsh and Indian descent who regularly judges on Food Network shows, including my favourite, *Iron Chef,* says he doesn't think so. In his 2011 book *Eating for Britain*, he called chicken tikka masala, which was most likely developed in Glasgow by a man who'd immigrated from Pakistan as a way to appeal to British palates, "as British as fish and chips." But he drew the line at trying chicken tikka masala lasagna, a featured special at a pub. "I'd probably try it now," Majumdar says. "I mean, there's a certain point where you might say, 'Let's stop.'"

"Looking at your recipe," he says, "you have red peppers and green peppers. Red peppers and green peppers come from Latin America. So where does that come from? You've got all this mixture there to create this thing called pickle. And the term 'pickle' comes from a German term, and from there a Norse term," he says.

The more food history he learns, Majumdar tells me, the more he lets go of authenticity.

When it comes to British and Indian cuisines, Majumdar points out that it's been a long relationship. The first Indian restaurant to open in Britain was the Hindoostane Coffee House in London in 1809 or 1810.

And it's a bidirectional relationship too. "Go and look up Indian sandwiches," Majumdar says. "If you go to Delhi, they have something called a pav bhaji, which is a bread roll filled with this tomato dal. There's a whole range of different types of sandwiches. They all have some pickles in them or some cheese in them, which wasn't really a part of Indian cuisine apart from the paneer cheese that they use for things like saag paneer. They'll put some pickles on top, which could be a tomato pickle or a green chutney, or whatever. And they'll usually toast them. There are dozens, if not hundreds, of Indian sandwiches now that have been there for, I'm guessing, probably around a hundred years." The idea of these sandwiches most likely came back to India with the British, Majumdar says. They're delicious. And neither side can quite claim them, but a hundred years seems like long enough to call them "authentic."

Or perhaps that term is somewhat futile anyway. "I've stopped thinking about authenticity," Majumdar says. "What I am thinking about now is 'Am I just enjoying it?' And that's how I think about any food I'm going to write about now. How am I enjoying it? And then from that, I'll start off on where it comes from."

Tomatoes, like peppers, are their own particular artifact of colonial movement and adoption and adaptation. In *Indian Food: A Historical Companion*, food historian K.T. Achaya writes that "there seems to be no record of when the tomato came to India." Thought to have originated in Mexico or Peru, he continues, it seems most likely that the tomato arrived in India by way of England in the late eighteenth century and was first cultivated to feed the foreign palates of the English, before eventually being adopted into sour curries by Bengalis and Burmans the following century.

Collingham describes a Bengali chutney she frequently makes at home: you heat a pinch of panch phoron, which consists of cumin seeds, nigella seeds, fennel seeds, wild celery seeds, and fenugreek seeds, in hot oil, and then you add minced ginger and garlic. After a few seconds, you add dried hot chilies. And then chopped tomatoes, some sugar and salt, cover, and let it cook down. At the end, she says, you add a big green chili or two, just so the spice comes out, and then some dried mango, so it reconstitutes, adding sweetness to the chutney. "That is just an absolutely wonderful chutney," she says. And a pretty standard Bengali fresh chutney.

In Britain, Collingham says, a pickle could be described as vegetables in a clear vinegary sauce; a chutney would be a bit messier, with everything incorporated and less distinguishable. But they'd both use vinegar, unlike the vast majority of Indian chutneys, relishes, and pickles.

My nana's chutney is pretty dissimilar to most South Asian tomato chutney recipes I find online, other than the tomatoes and the use of spices such as turmeric and cloves. It doesn't bloom its spices; it treats the tomatoes overnight with salt, uses vinegar, uses bell peppers rather than chilis. But it bucks British pickle trends, too, by using white sugar and white vinegar, alongside more familiar English pickle staples like tomatoes, apples, onions, and mustard.

It may not taste like Bengali tomato chutney, but it also tastes very unlike Branston Pickle, which is made using barley malt vinegar, sugar, apple pulp, tomato purée, date paste, and "vegetables in various proportions"—namely those that grow easily in the U.K. and have been around for a while: carrots, rutabaga, onions, and cauliflower.

In a *Spectator* article that makes a case for Branston Pickle as a national treasure, Ameer Kotecha writes, "There is something pleasing about its ugliness: brown and lumpy. A rebuke to Instagram. The unassuming appearance makes its delightful flavour all the more surprising: the vinegary tang, the gentle spice, the sweet fruitiness, all in perfect balance." (He also writes that Branston Pickle, which is a bit reminiscent of Bengali date and tomato chutney or Rajasthani sweet and sour lemon pickle, "has the hallmarks of Empire.")

To me, Branston Pickle tastes sweet in the way that molasses or treacle tastes sweet—with a profound bass, or umami, note. I don't like it.

When I first became curious about where my nana might have gotten her recipe, research led me to a type of chutney popular on the East Coast of Canada and in the southern United States. Called chow or chow chow (maybe after "choux," French for cabbage), some recipes for this chutney, maybe more aptly called a sweet relish, overlap quite a bit with my nana's. One recipe, billed as Southern Chow Chow and claiming regional coverage from Kentucky to Florida, says it will "take you a step back in time to Granny's kitchen." It uses white vinegar and sugar and very similar spices to my nana's and includes onion and green and red bell peppers. But it omits apples, contains four green tomatoes instead of twenty-four red tomatoes, and uses six cups of shredded cabbage, a vegetable that never came within a metre of my nana's chutney.

Collingham suggests a different origin. She wonders if what my nana made was adapted from another popular—but not quite as enduring as Branston Pickle—British chutney called piccalilli. "Instinctively," she says, "my sense is that it's probably coming out of both traditions. The desire to have sharp condiments with roast meat, which is a very old kind of Anglo desire. And then the actual pickling spice profile sounds like a tomato version of piccalilli. The spice profile could well have been influenced by Indian spices."

It sounds very similar, she says, to piccalilli recipes from the 1920s in sources like *Good Housekeeping*. When she was growing up in the 1970s, her granny might have made piccalilli. But she hasn't seen it at the stores or in anyone's kitchens for a while. (Incidentally, when Atkins confesses a dislike for Branston Pickle, he tells me he does like, and makes annually using vegetables from his garden, a mustard-forward variation of piccalilli.)

And it's possible that my nana made a tomato variation because wherever we grow tomatoes, we seek ways to preserve the summer glut of them, Collingham says.

As I end my research, I still don't have an answer. This is a field, Atkins tells me, that hasn't been terribly well researched yet. (Fleetingly, I consider the prospect of doing a food history PhD.) Though I don't have a definitive answer, I do have a variety of possibilities and lineages to consider. It's possible my nana ate piccalilli in England, brought a recipe over, and adapted it. It's possible my nana carried with her, like my dad's family did, the idea of eating cheese and chutney, was introduced to chow chow, and adapted that recipe based on what my grandfather grew in his garden and what they liked to eat. It's possible her recipe came from her mother. It's possible it came from a family she nannied for when she first came to Canada. It's possible she cribbed it from a magazine, either in the U.K. or in Canada. It's possible she saw it on the back of a bottle of vinegar. Who knows.

Ultimately, I'm okay with this uncertainty. And now I'm curious if my nana would have stopped making this chutney if I hadn't had such a voracious appetite for it. Which strikes me as a bit funny: as an unwitting working-class settler kid born in the 1980s in Canada, it's possible my affection for my grandmother and her chutney kept this condiment, with its tangled colonial roots, alive.

because someone
saved the seed

Kevin Wilson, who lives on about one-fifth of an acre in a striking two-tone blue house with a pride flag flapping gently in the breeze above the front porch, grows breadseed poppies and lovage and fennel and crocuses and narcissus. He grows lettuce and corn salad and comfrey. Several kinds of currant and an apple tree, called a maiden apple, that grows straight up rather than branching out. His specialty, though, is soup peas, a type of pea that's grown to dry and store and, as its name suggests, is mainly used for soup. He grows them for himself and to sell to friends and neighbours.

A mutual friend introduced us because she thought I'd learn a lot from Kevin, who also runs a homesteading school and forms part of a fairly large network of smaller-scale seed farmers and sellers in the Pacific Northwest. I'd been looking to learn more about what goes into the process of saving seeds to sell and grow; it had begun to feel, for me, like an inevitable offshoot of growing fruits and vegetables.

Understanding how different types of plants grow and go to seed is the first step towards learning how to save seeds at home and what it means when we're buying a packet at the store. Plants like kale and carrots, for example, are biennial, meaning they need to be overwintered and allowed to flower and go to seed in their second year. Some plants, like squash and cucumber and carrots, cross-pollinate fairly readily, meaning they need to be isolated from varieties that share the same family. Other plants, like tomatoes, are self-pollinators, meaning it's possible to grow different varieties in fairly close proximity. Plants like bell peppers need to be fully red and ripe before their seed can be harvested, which can be tricky due to climatic conditions in the Pacific Northwest. I often pick and eat mine when they're green because they're reluctant to redden, even in my greenhouse.

But there are other considerations involved. When I buy my Sweet Million cherry tomatoes, I'm buying a variety bred to be productive and disease-resilient. But they're hybrid seeds, created by intentionally cross-pollinating parent plants—meaning any seeds I save from the fruits won't be reliably similar to their parent plants. Should I be growing an open-pollinated variety instead, one that can adapt, over time, to climate change and my microclimate? The year I visit Kevin is one that will see a record-breaking heatwave and a perilously early start to wildfire season. So resilience is top of mind. How are ecologically minded growers and seed sellers adapting their practices to make small-farm and backyard crops more resilient? And what should growers be keeping in mind when we're buying the seeds we can't save ourselves?

Saving seed is a political act. Much of the food we buy from the grocery store is derived from seeds that have been genetically modified to tolerate herbicides and pesticides, increase nutrients, or increase disease and drought tolerance. In some cases, the food we buy is grown from "terminator" seeds—seeds developed by companies such as Monsanto, which are designed to produce plants that have sterile seed, so farmers are forced to buy new seeds from that company the following year. These same companies may also vertically integrate their seed-selling arm with their pesticide and fertilizer arms. They sue farmers aggressively to protect their seed patents. In short, their seeds are the kernel from which industrialized farming—with its strengths and its myriad weaknesses—grows.

Saving and sharing seed, then, defies the capitalistic pressure to hoard and monopolize. It feels more akin to what seeds themselves aim to do in the world. As physicist and activist Vandana Shiva has said, "Seed is created to renew, to multiply, to be shared, and to spread. Seed is life itself."

On an unseasonably warm and dry October day, I meet a handful of farmers from Stowel Lake Farm at a local agricultural hub called the Root, just over a kilometre from Ganges Harbour on Salt Spring Island. The Root, which is run by the Salt Spring Island Farmland Trust, has a commercial kitchen, food storage space, meeting space, and an office space. It also houses the Salt Spring Seed Sanctuary, a charitable organization dedicated to preserving and promoting open-pollinated heritage seeds. Its database contains 115 varieties; 577 members grow out seeds, reporting back on the performance of the plant and saving seeds from the best and strongest specimens. "Our mantra is that good food comes from good seed," they write in their summer 2022 newsletter.

Today, the Root is providing yet another service: it's teamed up with FarmFolk CityFolk to bring a mobile seed cleaner to the island for a couple days. When I arrive, a woman is using seed-cleaning screens to process her homegrown lentils. Soon, Meghan McEachern, Stowel Lake's head farmer, arrives with five or six other farmers and several Rubbermaid bins holding large paper bags full of seeds that need to be cleaned.

Siri van Gruen, who works at FarmFolk CityFolk, shows me the thresher, a red and beige machine that uses vigorous motion to split the pods and separate seeds from chaff. Siri places rye in the hopper. The seeds fall through a screen and pass out the side of the machine, through a chute, into a waiting blue Rubbermaid bin. The chaff is carried through the machine and spat out onto a waiting tarp. There are two screen sizes—a smaller screen useful for grain, and a larger one useful for beans. One of the more curious uses she's seen, she tells me, was for a buckwheat pillow maker whose focus was on getting the hulls rather than the seeds.

Thea, a farmer from Stowel Lake, attempts to use the thresher for radish seeds; although the seeds themselves are relatively small, they're enclosed in hard, puffy, tough-to-crack pods. The thresher turns out to be no match for the pods, so Thea turns to something called a threshing box: it's wooden with a ridged floor and is large enough to stand in. Thea steps on the radishes in her boots, crushing the stubborn pods as she grinds the balls of her feet in semicircles.

Siri demonstrates the Winnow Wizard next. This machine is larger with a hopper on top. Farmers from Stowel Lake feed it some spinach seeds. An auger in the hopper shakes the seeds loose from the pods. A fan—which is set to low for small seeds like spinach, and high for large seeds like beans—blows the chaff loose, and the seeds get funnelled into a wooden box. I'm not sure why, but I was expecting spinach seeds to look like kale seeds: small, dark, round. Instead, I find they look like little brown buckwheat groats. It is mesmerizing to watch the thresher and the Winnow Wizard at work. Despite the commotion, their work is delicate. And it's satisfying to see the seed pods processed so efficiently.

"You have a good amount of chaff in your hair already, Meghan!" someone—maybe Thea or Hannah—calls as the Winnow Wizard continues to do its work.

When Thea is done crushing radish pods, she uses a generator-powered air compressor to blow the chaff from the seeds in the box.

With the noise from the machines added to the physical separation they create, it's hard to hold a conversation, or sometimes to even tell someone is trying to talk. So after a half hour of taking notes, I settle into a spot on the Root's gravel parking lot with some manual seed-cleaning screens, slowly working my way through flower seeds. First up is Texas hummingbird sage, a type of salvia that guards its seeds in small pods that I break open by rubbing them over a metal screen with my hands and into a waiting wooden box. I move on to mixed cosmos, long thin seeds with similarly sized chaff, separated most easily by lightly blowing on the screen until it floats away on the breeze. And finally coreopsis, which also guards its seeds in a little pod at the base of the flower.

When the machines are quiet, I chat with the farmers from Stowel Lake. In addition to the spinach and radish, they're tackling mustard, arugula, chard, Amish peas, lettuce, scallions, and more. The scallion seed heads are surprisingly fluffy; I never would have guessed. Similarly, I never would have guessed I'd find seeds in general so magnetizing. But I do—each small seed contains its own comparatively massive world of potential.

Some seeds we save so we can sow the vegetables or flowers again. Others are dual purpose. The dried beans and peas we use in cooking are the same ones we'll plant next year. Celery seed, which tastes exactly like celery, can be used in potato salads and vinaigrettes, soups and chilis. The seeds of plants in the mustard family, also known as brassicas, like broccoli, can be used to make grainy mustards. Squash seeds can be roasted or toasted.

When plants like kale grow a flower stalk and go to seed, they shoot up to double or triple or quintuple their harvest-season height. The leaves of the plant become bitter as it turns its energy towards reproduction; at this point, it is taking up space in the garden in service of making future plants that will be harvestable, rather than continuing to be harvestable itself. Some plants, like celery—or again kale—produce an overwhelming amount of seed per plant, more than a home gardener would ever reasonably use themselves. Both start from seeds so small they can get lost in the creases of your palm. And then they grow, and they crop, and they produce thousands of new seeds. Each plant feeds us for a time and then provides us with an opportunity to feed ourselves and each other again the next year. It's all terribly mundane, but it's mundane in the way that all life cycles are simultaneously mundane and a type of embodied magic, full of love and grief. From the earth we all emerged, and to the earth we all will return again.

At the same time, it's all very practical. The machinery that FarmFolk CityFolk tours around the province allows home gardeners and small and mid-sized farms the ability to save labour by sharing machines and tools at a scale that makes sense for them—a half step between manual seed-cleaning screens and the giant combines used on large-scale farms.

This brings a lot of value to farms like Stowel Lake. Thea tells me she estimates this half-day they're spending at the Root with the mobile seed cleaner will save a month's worth of manual seed-cleaning work back at the farm.

Most farms I've visited, even small farms run by people heavily invested in local food and food security, do not build seed saving into their annual rhythm. It's time-consuming, takes up growing space, and can be tricky if it gets too cold or rainy too quickly in the fall. Stowel Lake is an outlier; I've come to Salt Spring to understand why and to see how they do what they do.

The next day, I reach Stowel Lake using a hand-drawn map Meghan sketched into my notebook. I cross a dry creek bed and an ornately carved wooden bridge that looks like something from the Shire in the *Lord of the Rings*. I pass by a house, through a gate, and down a lane. I walk by a field containing two white alpacas and an inquisitive brown cow relaxing in some lush grass. Eventually, the market garden comes into view: a gentle slope down into a small valley, the sun hitting the hill rising on the other side. There's an apple orchard, a wash station, an open-air seed propagating area holding pea sprouts that have just had a haircut. There are plastic-covered hoop houses and garden beds full of greens; there's a converted barn with rich brown wood and floor-to-ceiling windows in its loft. I am wearing a T-shirt and sunscreen; if the apples weren't near ripe on the trees, it would be hard to tell we're midway through autumn.

The farm is beautiful, verdant, idyllic. It's the type of place you visit once and immediately begin visualizing as a fantasy home. I hear people talking over in the wash station; when I approach, I see farmers Thea and Hannah, who direct me to the converted barn, which I learn houses the commercial kitchen, used to prepare meals for retreats, as well as the farm office and a loft space set up with dining and lounge areas.

Squash is curing under the skylights in the loft: red kuri, kabocha, carnival butternut, sweetmeat. If I lived here, I catch myself thinking, I'd work in the retreat kitchen, which smells like many vegetarian kitchens I'm familiar with: oats and cinnamon, roasted vegetables, cumin. While Meghan finishes up a few tasks, I gaze out the loft's tall windows, picturing myself turning farm greens into salad tossed in an herby vinaigrette; in the fall, using some homemade yogurt in a dough for an apple galette, topped with a drizzle of caramel.

When she's done, Meghan gives me a garden tour. As soon as we leave the converted barn, we run into Lisa, who bought this land in the mid-'70s and raised her family here. For a time, Lisa ran the farm as a U-pick strawberry farm. Now, she focuses on the perennial gardens, designing them so that there is something blooming year-round, providing nectar for birds and pollinators. The perennial garden has become something of a collection, Meghan tells me; Lisa grows some unusual, harder-to-find perennials, gleaning seeds and selling starts through the farm stand.

About twenty-five people live on the farm year-round, including eleven children ranging in age from two to seventeen. The farmers grow food for the retreat groups that come to the farm, for their community, and to sell at the farm stand. Unlike a lot of other market garden farms, they also grow plants for seed production.

The farm comprises about 120 acres in total, but the market garden is growing on about an acre and a half of land that sits in a low valley. This geography influences where crops are planted; a low mist comes in in the fall, Meghan says, making the area wetter and a bit colder. The hill, on the other hand, stays warmer and drier in the early spring and fall, so this is where they tend to grow plants destined for seed saving. There are pollinator beds planted around the food beds. In one area that Lisa has planted, redwing blackbirds are taking turns swooping in and harvesting seeds from a row of sunflowers.

They're intentional about which crops they grow for which purposes, Meghan says. For the farm store, they choose quick succession crops, like greens, that are ready to harvest in under seventy days. Crops like potatoes, squash, and onions, which take much longer to grow and ripen, are grown just for the community.

It's warm enough this October that tomatoes, eggplant, peppers, and basil remain in unheated hoop houses; fall crops like lettuce have now been planted at the base of the tomatoes and will continue growing after the tomatoes are taken out when it gets too cold for them. I try an herb I've never tried before, called tulsi. The leaves taste a bit sweet, a bit minty.

Meghan is carrying paper bags. In one field, we stop to harvest seeds from a Salvius romaine lettuce. We place the paper bags over the seed heads, bend the stalk of the plant, and shake. The seeds, surrounded by cottony fluff, flutter to the bottom of the bag.

Meghan points out some leeks growing—Lancia and Darcy's Purple. Eventually, she'll select the ones she wants to save and transplant them to the beginning of the row, to keep things tidy, concentrated, and easy to access.

There are still lots of plants in the ground, but much has been harvested, and Stowel Lake is now readying for winter. The zucchini will be pulled out soon; some beds will be mulched, and some will be tarped to keep the ground warmer and dryer for the crops to be planted in the spring.

We end our tour on the hill that rises on the opposing side of the valley from the converted barn. There are beehives, taken care of by a local beekeeper, Bruce. There are scarlet runner beans and bush beans. There are fruit and nut trees planted on a swale and berm system, on contour, for water management: hazelnut, apple, pear, peach, cherry, and olive trees. And there's a huge greenhouse—Lisa's new dream, Meghan says. It'll house subtropical trees, like citrus and avocado.

Over the years, Meghan says, Lisa has developed the farm with an eye to beauty. To me, it feels like Stowel Lake's seed saving is part of this: allowing plants to cycle all the way through their life stages instead of stopping them short also allows us to know them better, to pay a fuller kind of attention.

Larger companies, like West Coast Seeds, get around the problems of climate and seasonality by sourcing seeds from regions where the plants reliably grow well. Skagit County in Washington State, for example, is one of only two major growing regions in the world for spinach seeds, according to Mark Macdonald, West Coast Seeds' former communications manager.

On a visit to Skagit County, Mark once visited a warehouse for spinach seed producers. "They had these wooden boxes, four foot by four foot by four foot," he says. "And they'd be full of seeds. And there were ten of them tall, and fifty of them that way, and fifty of them that way. And that wasn't for one hundred years. That was for this season's spinach production. That's producing most of the world's spinach seeds."

"Many of us source from the same farm," Mark says. "And when those plants are ready to harvest the seeds, the farmers go out with their equipment and fill trucks, and the trucks line up for miles."

There's a stark difference between the scale of this type of spinach seed operation and what I saw at Stowel Lake, which saves seeds for their own growing purposes, as well as to package and sell through Salt Spring Seeds. The scale of the operation that West Coast Seeds taps into allows them to provide a massive amount of non-GMO, non-chemically-treated hybrid and open-pollinated seed reliably every year.

But growing seeds out through smaller-scale farms and via home growers, in conditions plant varieties find less than optimal, also forms a key part of long-term sustainability and food security plans.

Dan Jason, owner of Salt Spring Seeds and author of *Saving Seeds: A Home Gardener's Guide to Preserving Plant Diversity*, first got into seed saving and selling as an extension of his interest in practising self-sustaining, bioregional food growing. His perspective on dealing with climate conditions and diseases that make seed harvesting more difficult takes the long view.

"It's about navigating and taking advantage of situations that somebody else would look at as bad news," he says. "One year that I grew out three hundred different kinds of tomatoes, there was a very bad blight. And only a couple of tomato varieties survived it. So there you go: there's your opportunity to save blight-resistant tomatoes. That's a great opportunity."

Next to Dan Jason himself, Stowel Lake is the largest grower for Salt Spring Seeds. For seeds, they grow out three types of leeks; four types of beans; herbs like cilantro, parsley, and dill; greens like arugula, mustard, kale, spinach, and twenty varieties of lettuce; three kinds of peppers; peas; beets; radishes; two kinds of squash; and ten kinds of tomatoes.

"It's quite an orchestra," Meghan says. For each open-pollinated variety, Meghan tries to grow at least eighty plants in order to keep the genetic diversity healthy. When she grows the plants out for seed, she tries to balance the conditions she knows the plant prefers with those that are naturally available on the farm.

"We are looking at a climate reality where we are going to be struggling with drought in the future," Meghan says. "So it's crucial to see that we are working to grow seed that doesn't need as much water. Each year, we're really selecting and looking for those traits that can survive those kinds of climatic conditions."

In practice, this means she's experimenting with growing approaches. For the second year in a row, she's ensured spring-sowed seeds for crops destined for seed saving are given water to establish themselves in the spring but are not watered in the summer. "One of the varieties of lettuce did not develop seed because of that," she says. "Others did."

Within a variety, Meghan then zeroes in on which individual plants were most successful. "You're selecting the plants for which ones adapted—this one has done really well, this one hasn't." Saving the seeds from that plant, she hopes, will help develop adaptability in the next years' crops.

The importance of home growers to seed saving and seed diversity movements has also seen a recent resurgence. Seeds of Diversity, for example, has a thousand members coast to coast in Canada. Its seed library boasts over 2,900 regionally adapted and rare seed varieties; volunteer members grow out and multiply these seeds each year, helping to secure these varieties' futures. They also hold events called Seedy Saturdays, where home growers can share seeds and get seeds from other growers in their area—a way to try out new varieties with no cost outlay whatsoever.

Home growers don't often have the space to grow out dozens of examples of each plant, as Meghan might do at Stowel Lake, but they do have the freedom to grow out varieties that may not be as commercially viable, productive, or that have a smaller niche of people who prefer their characteristics. And this can lead to situations like Dan Jason saw with his blighted tomatoes—a surprising underdog variety can pull ahead in circumstances more popular varieties find too challenging.

When it comes to seed saving, both volume and diversity are important to ensuring food security in a changing climate; large farms, small farms, and home growers all have key roles to play.

While I'm on Salt Spring, I visit Dan Jason's farm too. The timing is not ideal; I haven't had cell service, and our plans were only tentative. But Meghan is heading over to drop off seeds (we packaged some French Breakfast radish and some Amish pea seeds when I visited the farm, as we were chatting), and I catch a ride. "It's not the time to talk about seed saving," he says when I arrive. "It's time to *do* the seed saving."

But he indulges me in a farm tour, and though I feel slightly guilty for imposing at a busy time of year, I'm grateful to see his seed cleaning and seed drying set-ups. In addition to writing about seeds and running Salt Spring Seeds, Dan is also the president of the Salt Spring Seed Sanctuary. He still does everything related to seed saving by hand; for large seeds like beans, he uses a threshing box and an air compressor to blow off chaff. For smaller, lighter seeds, he uses seed-cleaning screens.

His farm is on twenty-six acres, and he's been there twelve years. He grows out a large variety of seeds, everything from carrots to grains to legumes. In one greenhouse, Dan shows me black chickpeas, Utrecht blue wheat, and gaucho beans, a bush bean that's good to eat fresh as well as dried. All three are drying in the warm sun. In a second glass house, there are Lulu and Queen Sophia marigold seeds drying, and zinnia seeds and Nova aster. There are *Gaillardia* seeds that look like badminton birdies. There's triticale, a cross between rye and wheat; there's Black Einkorn wheat, and there are millet seeds, which resemble fuzzy caterpillars. Birds like the millet, Jason says, and you can get a lot of seed from one head. "When the birds start eating them," he adds, "you know they're ready to harvest."

Underneath the seed tables, there are lidded buckets partially filled with fermenting tomatoes: Graham's Good Keeper and Pollock, an early and productive variety. The fermentation process removes the protective natural coating around the seeds, which, while the fruits are growing, prevents them from germinating inside the tomato.

In 2019, Dan published *Changing the Climate with the Seeds We Sow*, which advocates that small growers turn their attention to beans, grains, herbs, and seed foods that haven't typically been grown widely in North America, at least on a smaller scale.

"I keep on telling people: if we're going to feed ourselves, it's okay to have carrots and beets and onions, but it's important to have the beans and grains that have fed us for thousands of years," he says. "Very few seed companies focus on grains and quinoa. But they're the easiest of all. They take minimal care and are the most rewarding."

I'm convinced: my next Salt Spring order contains Annie Jackson beans and a variety of bush bean called Early Pinkies. And—as I can't eat gluten and was aesthetically quite drawn to them in seed head form—it includes the millet I saw drying in Dan's glass house.

Speaking with seed growers and sellers gives me some real hope about mitigating the impacts of climate change—impacts that have been all around us in increasing ways the past few years, especially on the West Coast. It has also helped me better visualize the connections between what grows in my garden and its recent lineage.

By the time I said goodbye to Kevin Wilson at the end of his driveway last year, for example, I was taking home walking onions, lady's mantle, and a packet of Swedish Red peas, also known as Biskopens—a productive deep-burgundy soup pea he counts among his favourites. Now, the onions and the lady's mantle are thriving in our front yard. The Biskopens grew well in our backyard, and I saved enough for a few pots of soup and to grow more next year.

After I'd initially spoken with Dan and Meghan, I'd placed an order for seeds from Salt Spring, choosing at least one seed I knew would come from Stowel Lake Farms. Those plants I grew out the year I visited Salt Spring. I saved seeds from a variety of tomato I bought called King Umberto and from Sunshine Coast Fava beans.

Growing out seeds from the farmers and home growers I spoke with for this essay continues a cycle they began at their homes and on their farms, placing the plants I raise in a network that grows deeper and broader with each new grower. It takes a lot of care and attention to follow a seed from germination to production to the creation of its own seeds; each seed I have received is a gift that will continue and itself become a gift for someone else.

When I ask Meghan if farming for seed has changed her perspective on gardening and the growing process, she says it's expanded her view on ecology. "At every stage of a plant's life," she says, "it's not just the plant itself, it's also all of the pollinators, it's all of the other creatures and systems working around it which are working towards creating a plant at each stage."

It's also expanded the way she views seasons and the passage of time.

"Seeds are a multigenerational project," she says. "I'm not necessarily going to see all the fruits of what I'm doing today. You have to have a trust in the future, that actually what we're doing has benefit. And also that I'm inheriting all this work that people have done in the past.

"We are on the backs of thousands of years of seed savers and people who have adapted the varieties we eat today, for the characteristics that we're able to enjoy," she adds. "The only reason why we are able to eat the food we eat today is because someone has saved the seed."

vegan lemon macawrongs

On a grey day in mid-February 2022, after the first peak of Omicron has passed, my friends Nola and Megan come over to attempt vegan lemon macarons. (That is, the fancy little French sandwich cookies generally made with almond flour, icing sugar, and egg whites, not the desiccated coconut mounds.)

Sinclair has been wearing underwear on her head as a hat all day, and outside we're having a weeping tile installed around the perimeter of our house—every time it rains, water and mud seep into our basement, trailing miniature rivers along the concrete pad that separates the rest of the house from the dirt underneath and around us.

Nola is vegan and, like me, can't eat gluten. She's never tried a macaron before—a fact I find buoying, because if ours end up mediocre she will never know. Nola and Megan arrive bearing gorgeous bright-yellow lemons plucked directly from the tree growing in Nola's greenhouse.

My desire to perfect vegan macarons is one part social, one part food-driven, and one part ornery. Socially, the pandemic has left me lonely, and the idea of having two friends hang out in my kitchen to bake nearly brings me to tears. Food-wise, I want to provide Nola with a delectable morsel. And being ornery: one of my favourite-ever food essays is by Jeffrey Steingarten, and it's about his quest to make a perfect boudin noir after he eats one "at a dinner party just outside Paris," one so good he "quickly added it to [his] list of the hundred greatest foods of the world, tearfully removing the frozen Milky Way bar from [his] pantheon." Steingarten and I share a picky, snobby aesthete's love of food that is great, food that feels like a revelation, food that lodges itself in one's yearnings for life. (We also share a similar opinion about frozen Milky Ways—well, for me, Mars bars.) But my goal is to go on a *vegetarian* quest for perfection. I would like to see Nola's beautiful lemons turn into a delicately crunchy, beautifully chewy macaron, one that she can eat too.

We're using a recipe from the blog *Pies and Tacos*, which specializes in macarons and cupcakes, and seems to have done the most recipe testing of any of the bakers I can find online who have made vegan macarons. On the blog, Camila Hurst writes that she, like me, took up baking in part as a cure for depression—to find a hobby that would infuse her life with purpose and joy.

This recipe calls for aquafaba in place of the egg whites that would normally be used for the meringue that is folded with almond flour and icing sugar to make macaron shells. Aquafaba, as those of you who are vegan, vegan-adjacent, or allergic to eggs might know, is the liquid that surrounds canned chickpeas. The term was coined in 2015 by an American software engineer named Goose Wohlt, but the first known use of bean slime as an egg substitute came in December 2014, when Joël Roessel, a vegan opera tenor who wanted to eat île flottante, asked himself, according to the *Washington Post*, "What would disgust me as much as a raw egg white?"

Unlike Nola, I have made and eaten many macarons. I've eaten them in Paris. I've eaten them in Montreal and Vancouver and New York. I've eaten them fresh in my kitchen, deciding that I have spoiled myself for most commercial versions and can no longer purchase them from bakeries that only do them decently instead of really well. (Many bakeries use the Italian technique to make the meringue, which produces a more stable but drier cookie; many also seem not to use fresh flavourful almond flour. As a result, bakery shelves are often lined with macarons that feel like a sort of colourful sadness. Macarons made using the French technique for the meringue are liable to be visually imperfect but have a better chew and taste fresher.)

Pies and Tacos' recipe uses the Italian meringue method; I'm worried the aquafaba will be more finicky than egg whites, and I figure this is a safe place to start our trials. If it works well, I'll switch to French.

The aquafaba must be reduced to half of its volume by heating it in a saucepan. Half must then be used to make a marzipan-like paste with the almond flour and icing sugar, and the other half whipped to stiff peaks, to which I'll add sugar-water heated to 245 degrees Fahrenheit.

When I mix the marzipan with the meringue, the result is much stiffer than I'm used to. It takes muscle to complete the macaronage, and I don't get the batter to nearly the state I want. It feels like we could use it to spackle chips in our concrete basement floor.

Still, we pipe them and get them into a 210-degree oven just before five p.m. The recipe says they should take about thirty minutes to bake. It's been a journey to even get them here; we've made vegan vanilla buttercream and lemon curd too.

At 5:45 p.m., the macarons are nowhere near done. I place an order for takeout sushi.

At 6:10, when the macarons have been in for over an hour, I open the oven door and discover—though the shells look fine from the outside—that the insides of the macarons resemble angry lava.

We decide to bake them for a little longer. And then a little longer. At 6:30, after we've eaten sushi together, which in itself is nice—surprise dinner guests, kind of like when you're a kid and your parents acquiesce to an impromptu sleepover—we pull five specimens from the oven. One for me, one for Sinc, one for Will, one for Megan, one for Nola. We scoop out the molten centre and pipe vegan buttercream and lemon curd into the dry empty shells. They're . . . weird. Nola and Megan go home, and Sinclair goes to bed.

By 9:45, I decide that this first batch of shells, though they haven't yet dried out, can't stay in the oven any longer. I have a plane to catch the next morning. I decide to let them hang out on the counter overnight with a tea towel draped over them and pipe them if they've dried out by the time I wake up. They do not dry out. They are the worst thing I've ever attempted to bake, and a prickly sensation comes over me, a sensation that I have perhaps bitten off more than I can chew.

Attempt two: Friday, December 9, 2022.

This time, Nola comes over solo, and we use a French macaron technique from a blog called *Bakes and Blunders*, which does not require us to cook down the aquafaba. It isn't lemon season, so we don't have beautiful lemons to use from her tree.

The first part goes well. The aquafaba whips up and folds nicely into the almond flour and icing sugar. We make the same lemon curd we made last time; it works well, too, even with grocery-store citrus. The bright lemon flavour feels a little like splashing cold water on your face.

I've been poring over vegan macaron recipes, and the recipes have impressed upon me that I should not overmix the batter.

I am not looking to get to the stage of macaronage I would for traditional macarons, where the batter falls from my spatula in near-smooth ribbons. The batter that whips up for this attempt is closer to what I'm familiar with—just a little thicker. But the macarons still don't settle into a smooth shell. Instead, they retain ridges that remind me a bit of the poop emoji.

Still, they seem promising as a second attempt. We let them rest for fifty minutes on the counter, until the vast majority feel dry to the touch—no batter comes away on my fingertip when I press them lightly. In climates that are not as punishingly moist as ours, this step takes half as long.

I put them into the oven at 250 Fahrenheit for twenty minutes, rotating every five minutes. They rise and get a foot—the little band of waffly ridges at the base of the cookie. And then too large a foot: worrisome.

These shells end up completely hollow and fragile: another fail. We eat some of them, and I send Nola home with the lemon curd and a jar of broken macaron shards.

I have gathered some ideas for the next try: longer rest, lower oven temperature, and slightly more mixing, but just slightly.

Attempt three: Sunday, December 18, 2022.

This time, I make the macarons alone. I pulse my granulated sugar, hoping to make it finer, more like caster sugar. I fold the aquafaba meringue and almond flour and icing sugar together for longer this time, taking it almost to the ribbon stage before putting it in the piping bag. When I pipe the shells, they spread better, but I can tell my batter is still a bit too firm, still a bit undermixed. In other words, I know that the third time will not be the charm.

I let the shells rest on the countertop, where they are briefly investigated by my cat, Mackerel, who is confused—I'm also making miso soup, and the kitchen smells like dashi—but does not try to abscond with anything. The shells take about forty minutes to be fully dry to the touch.

This time, I put them into the oven at 200 degrees Fahrenheit, rotating them every ten minutes. I think they'll be done at thirty minutes. They are not. I take them out at forty minutes and can tell that they are hollow. But, I think, maybe they'll be workable anyways? They are still not workable. The feet are smaller than last time. The shells lift off the Silpat more evenly. But they are still molten inside, more like a grainy marzipan than a macaron. I text Nola: "I think they'd be good on vegan ice cream?"

I'd baked gluten-free chocolate chip cookies that weekend. The night before making the macarons, we'd had black beans, squash, and tomatoes on polenta, a meal composed of ingredients almost entirely grown in our yard. And still I had to remind myself that I chose to take vegan macarons on in part because I knew they'd be a challenge, and that I'm failing not because I am a terrible, useless, no-good person who can't even get one thing right, but because the proteins in aquafaba are weaker than those in egg whites and that it's a bit zany to be attempting this in the first place. When I ask aloud, mostly rhetorically, what I am doing wrong, Will deadpans, "Making vegan macarons."

"On the upside," Nola texts, "it's good for your word count."

Attempts four and five: Sunday, February 26, 2023.

It's been a year since my first try. In the intervening months, I've made cakes, ice cream bars, trifles, baked Alaskas, eclairs, fried doughnuts, choux pastry, pizzas, breads—lots of technical stuff, all gluten-free. I've made Italian meringue for a s'mores cake; I've perfected my Swiss meringue buttercream and used it to frost a half-sphere cake I then painted with food colouring gels to resemble the planet Jupiter. I've even made more perfectly fine macarons with egg whites. What I have not yet succeeded at is this cursed recipe.

In this attempt, I make two batches. The first, the same as before but with more macaronage and a longer rest time. The second, using two grams less aquafaba, because I'm curious if the moisture held in the ingredients in our damp climate has been throwing things off. For the second batch, I also make some mini macarons, wondering if a smaller size will help.

The first batch, like all my previous batches, is curiously ridged. The second batch, with slightly less aquafaba and taken to the ribbon stage, finally pipes like a proper macaron. Unlike the others, it also looks like a proper macaron on the Silpat. I leave both batches to rest and develop a skin for an hour each. But both batches have the same hollow shell, exploded feet, gooey hellhole centre issue I've had since the beginning.

Today, while I'm making the macarons (or, to use the parlance of those in the macaron community, macawrongs), I deep clean my kitchen and make jambalaya for dinner. My best friend, Kim, says that when you bake, you still also have to cook. And when you fail at cooking, you still typically have something edible, something that will sustain you and that you never have to think about again. But baking offers us the opportunity to fail spectacularly while gaining no core sustenance whatsoever. At least, in this case, I've been wasting bean water rather than egg whites.

Attempt six: Monday, February 27, 2023.

On Monday morning, with the self-imposed March 4 deadline of this essay looming, I wake up at seven a.m. and walk up the hill to the local grocery store. The world is covered in a light dusting of snow that reminds me of icing sugar, because I have spent a lot of time lately sifting icing sugar into bowls with almond flour. And it's almond flour I'm heading out to buy. One of my new theories is that I need to be more particular about the almond flour I use, which, until now, has been the store brand. I've been pulsing it together with the icing sugar in the food processor a few times before running it through a sieve; maybe pulsing it is releasing almond oil and messing with the chemistry of the macarons? I buy a bag of Bob's Red Mill Super-Fine Almond Flour that costs almost twenty dollars. I also buy four more cans of chickpeas, no salt added.

That night, right after work, I start my sixth attempt. I decide on using the Swiss technique, which involves cooking down the aquafaba with granulated sugar before whipping it up into a meringue. I find the recipe on a blog called *Project Vegan Baking*, run by a London-based vegan named Tom. The macarons pictured on the blog are quite visibly textured in the shell, and the example recipe contains no food colouring, so they're a natural almond colour. But the recipe catches my eye for its precision, offering a number in grams for the amount I should cook my aquafaba and sugar down to. I calculate the weight of the pot and the initial weight of the contents, doing a bit of back-of-the-napkin math to figure out what pot plus half will equal. As it's cooking, I place the pot onto the scale periodically to check.

The other variable that has been keeping me up at night is my oven temperature. Something has felt off. The macaron shells I pipe following Tom's recipe are thick, thicker than his, and he suggests leaving them to rest for an hour. While they rest, I calibrate my oven with an oven thermometer. When the oven display reads 250 degrees, the oven thermometer reads about 295. My oven has been betraying me. Setting it at 225 or 230, I discover, gets me much closer to 250. Normally I would feel frustrated. But I find myself hopeful instead: better control of my oven temperature might lead to better results.

The first tray I bake are mini macarons. Tom's recipe suggests leaving them in the oven for a whopping forty minutes and then turning off the oven and leaving the door cracked open for an hour to let them dry out. So I do. During the baking stage, the macarons lift prodigiously—but then a bit too high, and lopsided.

Still, when I open the oven and take a mini mac off the Silpat, it lifts cleanly. It is not an unappealingly heated marzipan. It is a macaron. An *imperfect* macaron, but a macaron nonetheless. I text Nola and tell her I'll actually have a piped batch for her tomorrow, the first I've ever been able to produce. I feel like crying with joy. I also feel like cursing the macarons out: Take that, you little fuckfaces, I finally got one over on you.

The second batch, which are regular sized, take forty-five minutes to bake. By now, it is somehow 11:30 p.m. So when I turn off the oven, I leave the door propped open with the macarons in there and go to bed. In the morning, I check on them: they're still there, they peel off the mat easily, and they have large feet. They are somewhat hollow and look as though they came straight out of a cement mixer, but when I test one—sandwiching it with vegan lemon curd and some vanilla Swiss meringue buttercream I take out of my freezer—it rings the macaron bell in my brain. Finally—finally! I have made something resembling a passable vegan macaron.

After work, I engage Will's and Sinclair's help to make dinner—soba noodles in a miso broth with roasted broccoli, sweet potatoes, and chickpeas—while I make a vegan vanilla buttercream in the stand mixer and then painstakingly match up the slightly wonky macaron shells, filling them with curd and frosting. Again, I text Nola: this time, pictures of the filled macs. I'm excited for her to try them.

In Steingarten's boudin essay, he travels to France to learn how to make a boudin from start—butchering the pig—to finish, canning the boudin. After making the boudin, he and the cooks and farmers who butchered the pig eat a celebratory meal they call a fête du cochon, and Steingarten writes that "all [he] wanted to do after lunch was stagger into a soft bed and lose consciousness for a day or two." And yet tomorrow I'll face more emptied-of-aquafaba cans of unsalted chickpeas to use in some kind of meal—maybe braised with lemon, over quinoa and sweet potato purée? Will and Sinclair and I are beginning to tire of meals featuring unsalted chickpeas.

After making his boudin under tutelage, Steingarten returns to France to try again, this time just with his friends. The group begins the project at nine a.m. and finishes sealing the boudin in cans at seven p.m. By that time, Steingarten writes, they are "staring listlessly into space." They must then boil their sealed cans for three hours. Before leaving Paris for New York, Steingarten and his friends try their boudin noir. "We were in heaven, at least at first," he writes. "Our more mature judgment was that the taste and texture were nearly perfect, but that there was a bit too much blood in proportion to meat."

I'd remembered only the pleasure and satisfaction he described in this essay—a simple if obsessive and monied journey undertaken with more resources than I generally have access to, fresh Canadian lemons aside. And so when I first started making vegan macarons last winter, I assumed it would take a couple tries and then I'd have a new skill I could break out from time to time to make gifts for friends who don't or can't eat eggs. But this hasn't been the case. Instead, the quest has activated the part of my personality that was disappointed when I got 90 percent on a math test. I'd forgotten about the feeling that takes root when you go on a quest for perfection and can't quite reach it.

And I realized that the quest, which started out with friends, turned into somewhat of a lonely, quixotic venture. In some ways, it was more fun to fail in a group than to begin to succeed alone, even if what I was undertaking was in service of a friend.

Still, I am tempted to try another round of vegan macarons immediately. But I'm worried that if I remake them and they aren't an improvement on my most recent batch, I'll ruin my desire to ever make them again. Reading some *Serious Eats* trials run by Nik Sharma, I learn that canned chickpeas made with kombu, which contains carrageenan, makes the meringue, and thus the macarons, more stable. Part of me wants to wake up early tomorrow and head back to the store for chickpeas made with kombu. But I decide to keep that in mind for next time and choose to be satisfied for now; I'll wait until Nola's birthday rolls around, and I have an excuse to try a chocolate batch.

And it turns out I don't have to worry all that much about Nola and her partner Jason's reactions to the mediocre, just-passable macarons. "They're for *us*?!" Jason asks Nola, seeing my process posts on Instagram. Picking them up from our house, Nola tries one and loves it—satisfaction! Later that evening, she texts: "Jason is flipping out over the cookies!"

For me, this offers a lesson I'll need to keep learning. It's the opposite of what made me want to mimic Steingarten: not only can there be pleasure without animal products, there can be pleasure without perfection.

the spins family
board game

The restaurant where I learned to make yogurt did not
make most of its food in-house. The curries were made the
next town over and driven over in two-gallon pails, much of it
Northern Indian fare: matar paneer, chana masala, rajma, butter
chicken. We made onion bhajis and vegetable pakoras and rice
in-house, and we made yogurt by heating up milk in a large pot
on a hot plate, letting it cool to room temperature, and whisking in high-quality plain yogurt with a strong enough culture to
transform the whole pot.

The restaurant was called Curry in a Hurry, and it was located
in downtown Guelph in a century-old house next door to the
Guelph Mercury. Before I ever worked there, I ate there with my
dad. Our server was usually Tim, an energetic, outgoing dude
who seemed so at ease with himself, the kind of person who
coheres a group.

It was Tim who later taught me how to make yogurt. And
onion bhajis. The onions, the batter, the spicing, the ratio of
batter to onions—just enough to coat, so the bhajis would come
out looking like friendly edible spiders. We did the whole process with our hands. And then we'd drop the bhajis into hot oil

for the first time, cooking them just enough so they'd be ready to become golden brown and hot to order on their second fry.

Our job mostly consisted of reheating curries for people dining in and people ordering takeout. There was prep work in addition to making bhajis and pakoras and yogurt and raita— you could add green peppers or tomatoes or peas or raisins to your base curry for a small fee. But for the most part, it was a choreographed dance of microwaves and dishwashing. We adjusted the spice level of the dishes using cayenne pepper; one of the most popular recurring pranks we played on each other was to tip a pinch into a co-worker's almost-finished Diet Coke, offering them a little wake-up kick.

After I worked at the restaurant for a while, the apartment above it went up for rent, and I moved in with my then-partner and his childhood friend. Eventually, they worked at Curry too. After shifts, we drank at a bar a street over called the Jimmy Jazz. Smoking indoors was no longer legal in Ontario, but there was a loophole in the bar's back patio, which was semi-covered by an arbour and set up with wooden benches and teetering tables propped up by layers of weathered cardboard coasters. We drank pitchers of beer and, on Tuesdays, two-dollar mixed drinks.

By then, I was in my early twenties. I vacillated between overachieving and crashing and burning. High grades were then the primary way I understood myself as having value in the world. But I often felt like a garbage person. Classes had easily understandable rules; some were university-wide, and others classroom- or instructor-specific, and after settling in for a couple weeks, I understood these rules. But the unstructured time between classes—in hallways, in professors' offices, in social situations—were crevasses. I knew I could not be myself, not unless I was up to performing a version of myself that was funny or palatable through studied self-deprecation. Some of the things that had happened in my childhood felt unspeakably shameful. I'd meant to escape them and then did not; my partner had become an alcoholic, much like my mother was, and I again felt like I had to hide that reality from polite society. Much of my interior life, and my coping mechanisms, felt out of bounds.

In the small kitchen of the restaurant, however, heating up curry and deep-frying pakoras and bhajis and gently whisking yogurt into warm milk, I did not owe my co-workers sanity. They ribbed me lightly for wearing closely related iterations of the same bargain-basement outfit every day, saying I resembled a cartoon character. We listened to the same CBC shows regularly, mixing them in with albums we could agree on: Modest Mouse's *The Moon & Antarctica*, the Streets' *Original Pirate Material*. I was fucked up, I knew that. But they all were too. In ways I could recognize. In ways that let me be at ease, be the person I was then.

We were also all chronically broke. Towards the ends of our shifts, if we'd made enough tips, we pooled our money and sent someone to the liquor store for Forty Creek whisky or vodka, usually Stoli. And we smoked a lot of pot. I stopped around the time I went on lithium—you are definitely not supposed to take recreational drugs while on lithium. I did start smoking Belmont Milds, though, often bumming them off Tim so I could avoid feeling like I was really a smoker.

A few summers earlier, when I'd had my first hypomanic episode, which landed me in the ER, I was working three jobs. My Parks and Rec gig—which expected me to arrive at the same early time every day, be pleasant to park visitors, and leave at the same dinner hour daily—became too much. But the others, food service gigs with variable schedules, I could do even while coming off a combination of Paxil and benzodiazepines—I was on two, one for panic attacks and one for chronic anxiety—cold turkey.

That fall, when I returned to school, I was too poor not to work. As I adjusted to a new regimen of medications, processed the chaos and trauma of the preceding summer, started second-year university courses, and discovered that cognitive behaviour therapy and group therapy were not going to work for me, I searched for jobs. Specifically for jobs in food service, working in the kitchen. I knew a kitchen was a place I could work while I was not fit to be seen by the public. And that's when I found Curry. As long as I showed up, worked my shifts, and fulfilled my duties, I would get my cheque and pay my rent and buy my groceries—even as I was having my blood taken regularly to measure its level of lithium. And even as I was still regularly hallucinating—hearing voices and seeing birds indoors, in places they could not have been.

Much has been written and said about how kitchens are unsafe places for women and queer people and racialized people, shot through with cruelty and harassment—in particular if the kitchen follows the strict hierarchical structure of fine dining, adopted from the French tradition. Kitchens also underpay workers, compounding that underpayment with wage and tip theft. But like many things in life, it's more complex than that. Kitchens, in particular those that don't pretend any affiliation with anything approaching fine dining, can be very safe places to land for the world's weirdos. They're always hiring (so it's easy to leave and go elsewhere), no one gives a shit what you look like, and if you are battling some personal demons, you're generally not alone. In fact, if you're used to dysfunction, they can feel very much like a second home.

One night it was snowing heavily. Curry was very slow, take-out orders only, and my partner created an entire board game designed to help us get drunk. He called it the Spins Family Board Game. One square required us to throw frozen peas into a red solo cup from across the room, taking a shot for every pea that missed the cup. Another had us turn in circles, our foreheads pressed to a baseball bat. Every time a delivery driver or customer came in to pick up an order, we were temporarily quiet. After they left, we resumed the game.

Sometimes at Curry, I joined in when everyone drank, and sometimes I went home alone and studied. And sometimes I was uptight, short-tempered with my friends for drinking so much, when really the problem was that I wanted to be surrounded by sobriety but didn't know how to seek it. Innocent and a bit naive, according to Tim. And often the voice of reason, though usually everyone ignored me.

The night of the Spins Family Board Game, I got as drunk as anyone. I spilled curry all over my off-brand Crocs and ran them through the dishwasher at the end of the night with the slip-resistant commercial kitchen mats. I don't remember leaving work or going upstairs to sleep. I remember feeling woozy and finding it funny—it was the essence of his charm—that my partner had named the game so presciently. In retrospect, it marked a turning point, a night when things had gone a bit too off the rails, inebriation seeping too late into the worknight. This would become something my partner would lean into, and something I'd break from, afraid of losing any more control over my life.

But we really did feel like family. Tim was like my wild yet protective older brother. My co-worker Ali, whose favourite line when training people was "There is no right way," was also a bit like an older sibling. Or maybe a twin I loved even though one of us had emerged wound tighter than a cake made with no leavening and the other as relaxed as high-hydration ciabatta. We were stuck together, often close and sometimes resentful. Usually caring, sometimes enabling. Spinning, but spinning together.

After writing the first draft of this essay, I wondered if my friends had known that I had been emotionally in the nadir of my life, that they had formed part of the small web of relationships that kept me afloat. So after a long period of procrastination—I felt anxious about reaching out—I asked them.

Tim told me that food service had offered him a lot of the same things it had offered me. "I could maintain a job through my mental health issues and addictions," he told me: "Not starting until eleven a.m. can make doing drugs until sunrise a reality."

Ali was the parent of one baby when we finally reconnected on the phone for the first time. It was a busy afternoon, and our conversation was very soon interrupted by the arrival of a delivery at her tree nursery job. And then by the time we talked again, she was the parent of two. I got the sense from Ali—and Tim told me directly—that when they reflect on our time together at Curry, they feel some shame, alongside love and care.

Tim put it better than I could, texting, "I felt safe and seen when we were all out forgetting together."

It's reassuring to me that Tim feels a similar mix of emotions as I feel. I tell him about a concept my friend Sigal developed, something called the "scarf of absolution." Someone waves it for you, I tell him, and you're absolved. Maybe we can all wave it for each other.

The complicating factor for all of this is that I can't get back in touch with everyone I'd like to; I'll never know exactly what this time felt like for them, or how they see it now. One of the people I was really close to doesn't have an internet presence anymore, and I'm not sure what it means that he fell off the radar. Another, I do reach out to a few times when I stumble across his profile on Facebook—but I don't hear back. A mutual friend tells me he went to rehab. Maybe me popping up is like poking a bruise. Maybe it provokes too much anxiety. Maybe I hurt him somehow, in a way I don't remember in the haze of time. Maybe the same things that kept me afloat pulled him under. I'm not sure, and it's unfair to guess.

After I left Curry, the Spins Family Board game continued on as Family Social, adding new mini games like BLUT (Believable Lie or Unbelievable Truth) and feats of strength. Ali rented a house with her brother and cousin, and it had an open-door policy, and I was there a lot. We fed each other, ran errands together, did the crossword, spent too much money, remained chronically broke.

I got a job in communications after I graduated, broke up with my partner, and then got an additional part-time job in another kitchen. Eventually, most of us who'd worked at Curry found our way out of the hot, humid environment of kitchens altogether—into trades, into horticulture, into publishing. It wasn't a linear path for me, and when I moved across the country a couple years later, I shed almost everything that connected me to Guelph, as much of it felt too painful to hold on to.

To this day, I keep the option of food service tucked away in my mind as an if-everything-goes-wrong plan C. When I couldn't bother dressing myself, when I was at my most unwell, I could still work in a kitchen. I placed food at the top of my pyramid of needs, jettisoning much of what most other people considered necessary and retaining it well after I let other basic daily requirements fall through the cracks.

Even now, when I'm too depressed to talk or think or write or do anything else, as I am intermittently during the writing of this book—in summer and fall 2022, when my brain feels like it's been stripped of serotonin, and my body of energy and affect—I can still cook. I cook when I'm so exhausted that I need to take breaks to lie down while things are in the oven. When the harvest starts in the garden, and it takes me two hours to pull a simple sentence out of myself, I can prep and cook and bake all day. I listen to audiobooks and reach a kind of affectless peace.

This is due in part to the small but satisfying achievement of taking disparate ingredients and turning them into a meal. But it's also because the people I've worked with in kitchens have allowed me to be myself, nowhere more than at Curry.

Revisiting my memories, I want to revisit the food too. For the first time in years, I make yogurt at home. I buy a bunch of onions and a jug of oil, and mix the batter for bhajis. I let the oil get hot in an enamelled cast iron pot fitted with a thermometer. The feeling of the batter on my hands as I incorporate the onions is as familiar as Ali's voice was on the phone. When I drop the bhajis into the oil, working quickly, I watch and listen, satisfied, as hundreds of tiny steam bubbles froth to the surface. My kitchen fills with the smell of frying onions, cumin, chickpea flour.

The act of making them conjures the past. And when I dip a bhaji in tamarind chutney and take a bite, it feels as if I am bringing a small piece of my former self forward in time and offering it the unconditional acceptance my co-workers offered me when I wasn't able to offer it to myself.

consider the carrot

When I was a child, my family tells me, I ate so many carrots straight from my grandfather's garden that my palms started to turn yellow. My brother and I were dropped off at my grandparents' house every weekday morning in the summers when we were in elementary and middle school. Every year, my granddad rototilled an eighth-of-an-acre patch in their backyard, adding compost and growing asparagus, zucchini, tomatoes, lettuce, carrots, leeks, strawberries. They had a plum tree and a pear tree, under which some of our family photos were taken over the years. If my nana was watching, we'd run the carrots under the water of the hose at the back of the house. If she wasn't, my grandfather would gesture at me to brush the dirt off on my pant leg.

The carrots we ate inside, at lunch, were still carrots from the garden, but they were carrots my nana had peeled, cut into sticks, and placed into a glass with water in the bottom to keep them fresh. This glass also usually contained celery and cucumber. In a rectangular Tupperware fitted with a plastic screen at the bottom, she kept the as-yet-uncut backup vegetables, wrapped in damp paper towels.

At the time—still—I loved rabbits, who ate from everything in the garden, leaving little nibbling bites on the lettuce. My granddad often threatened to purchase a pellet gun to show the rabbits what was what. *Rabbit stew!* he'd yell. *You'll be rabbit stew!* And I'd protest, and my nana would say, *Phil!* And the rabbits and their sets of four ever-growing teeth would live on, feasting.

As I got older, carrots became a different kind of cornerstone in my life. When I first moved away from my childhood home, my parents weren't able to help me financially, and I didn't want to ask my grandparents, who were, I guessed, already helping my parents; student loans, after tuition, left me about five thousand dollars a year to supplement my earnings from the part-time jobs I worked while going to school full-time. The first year was rough, but the following years were worse—my grip on stability loosened further after I was diagnosed bipolar at eighteen. It felt like a feat just to survive, and looking back, I'm not sure how I did.

My friend Jane and I shopped at the No Frills together, which was a city bus ride away. Our staples were eggs, tins of baked beans and diced tomatoes, oatmeal, potatoes, rice, pasta, beans and pulses, carrots, apples, and bananas. These carrots were not like the carrots my grandfather had grown, delicate and fresh. These carrots had peels that had gone pale with age in places. Middle-aged carrots that had clearly spent some time in a special carrot storage facility to extend their lifespans. Raw, they were a bit bland, and a bit hard on the jaw to crunch, but passable. Cooked, they added bulk to pastas, and rice and bean meals, and soups—basically whatever we were making.

The memory of carrying carrots and canned foods in bright yellow bags, their handles elongating under the weight of our heavy grocery staples, is as bright and consistent as the memory of my grandfather showing me how to pull a ready-to-harvest carrot

from the soil he amended specially to grow them straight and true.
I guess what I'm saying is that carrots have range.

Carrots are in the parsley family. They're biennial plants, meaning
they flower in their second year, and their pollination is assisted
by insects like bees, hoverflies, houseflies, and bluebottles. If you
let them flower and go to seed, they look remarkably like Queen
Anne's lace: clusters of tiny white flowers radiate out from small
stalks in an umbel pattern, looking sort of like a cross between a
doily and an umbrella. The carrots we eat (*Daucus carota* subsp.
sativus) look remarkably like Queen Anne's lace (*Daucus carota*
var. *carota*) because they're quite closely related to Queen Anne's
lace, which is also known as wild carrot.

Carrot seeds, says Dan Jason, author of *Saving Seeds* and
owner of Salt Spring Seeds, are very easy to harvest. The flower
the plant sends up in its second year contains hundreds of tiny,
easily accessible seeds. To collect them, you just need to place a
paper bag over the flower head and shake until the seeds rain
into it.

"The hard thing is to make sure the seed is pure," Dan says.
The conventional wisdom online says that if you live within a
mile or so of a plant, it's difficult to grow carrots for seed. If
you try, they can end up cross-pollinating. In Washington State,
Queen Anne's lace is classified as a class B noxious weed, and
it's prohibited to sell or transport its seeds. Thankfully, there's no
Queen Anne's lace in the valley where his farm is located, and
so he's safe to save carrot seeds.

The taproots of Queen Anne's lace, technically edible when
they're very small and young, become woody and bitter as the

plant matures. If you pick Queen Anne's lace or brush it with your hand, it smells temptingly carroty. But if your carrots cross-pollinate, they'll most likely pick up the traits we want least in carrots (toughness, woodiness, bitterness).

David Catzel, the BC Seed Security Program manager for FarmFolk CityFolk, tells me that carrot seed saving is slightly more complicated than distance between carrots and Queen Anne's lace. The insects that pollinate both plants, he says, can travel up to five kilometres, not just a mile. But, he says, "the carrots can be right by Queen Anne's lace if it doesn't flower right at the same time."

"Isolation by distance is just one factor," David tells me. "Exact distance is a guideline that changes depending on the landscape. A farmer's lived experience with isolation on their farm is more relevant than suggested numbers in a book."

David also raises another consideration for carrot seed saving. If you're seed saving from plants like lettuce, tomatoes, beans, and peas, you can harvest from five plants each year for generations and suffer no hardships. But for long-term genetic health for carrots, you need to be harvesting from about a hundred plants—a little trickier as a home grower.

Carrots are still one of my top five all-time favourite foods. Even a bad carrot—one gone a *little* woody, or one whose flesh has separated from its core—is still a useful carrot in something like a stew or a soup, where it will be cooked so long that it picks up flavour and moisture, and no one will notice. But a truly good carrot is a thing of beauty. Sweet and crunchy, unfussy and welcoming. They're one of the few foods I can eat every day and never tire of. And I'm not alone: according to the UN's Food and Agriculture Organization, just under 41 million tonnes of carrots and turnips (the organization combines the two) were grown worldwide in 2020, the most recent year for which data's available. (This isn't quite as impressive as potatoes, 359 million tonnes, but it's more than pumpkins, squash, and gourds, coming in at just under 28 million tonnes.)

The first piece of writing the title of this essay harkens back to is M.F.K. Fisher's book *Consider the Oyster*, which is part biology lesson, part diatribe on whether oyster-related food poisoning is all it's made out to be, and part recipe book. "Love and Death among the Molluscs," its first essay, describes in detail the life cycle of an oyster from its imagined perspective. Another begins by citing a gravestone: "C. Pearl Swallow. He died of a bad oyster."

The second piece of writing this essay gestures towards is David Foster Wallace's "Consider the Lobster," about the Maine Lobster Festival and about lobster fishing and lobster etymology, but probably best known for its exploration of one central question: "Is it all right to boil a sentient creature alive just for our gustatory pleasure?"

On the surface, talking about growing and eating carrots might not seem as interesting, because they're plants—as in most agriculture, with the potential for exploitative labour practices; ecologically not so bad, at least not any worse, than other forms of conventional plant-based agriculture. Fewer ethical questions about plucking and boiling.

But I think they deserve a closer look because they are so popular, so well eaten, such a cornerstone of our diets. And so full of contradictions: somewhat tricky to grow at home, but relatively easy in commercial farm settings; potentially high-barrier in terms of cross-pollination, but if you manage to sidestep that, each umbel produces somewhere around a thousand extremely tiny seeds, easy to harvest.

And if you're drawn in by the morbid (I too often am): their consumption has killed at least one person I could find, a man who died in the 1970s of cirrhosis of the liver, his skin bright yellow, after consuming "a gallon of carrot juice a day" on top of millions of units of vitamin A.

On the internet, until very recently, there was a website called the World Carrot Museum, run by an English man named John Stolarczyk. As of December 2022, @CarrotMuseum was still tweeting—carrot-related content, but also a heady mix of pro-police and pro-Crown content—but the last snapshot of the website seems to have been captured by the Internet Archive Wayback Machine in late September 2022.

I learned about this website from Brody Irvine, who works in purchasing at Discovery Organics, an organic distributor that, where possible, purchases locally; he told me the website featured an "incredibly detailed" page, "almost like a novel," about baby carrots.

It also includes several detailed pages of carrot history, and it's where I learned that carrots were most likely cultivated over hundreds of years and initially domesticated in Afghanistan about five thousand years ago. That the earliest domesticated varieties were most likely purple, with some yellow variations, or maybe white, and the roots were much thinner than we see today. That it took hundreds more years to develop fatter, sweeter, non-forking carrots. That in the Middle East, carrots got bigger and better and more delicious but are still more often purple, from anthocyanins, the same pigment that makes red cabbage reddish-purple. And that the orange carrot originated in northern Europe in the late fifteenth century, most likely by

selectively growing yellow variations until they became progressively more orange, from beta-carotene.

Orange carrots are less prone to bolting than purple carrots
but do need—which I knew from reading extracurricular-to-
museum materials—a period of cold weather to bolt and flower
the following spring, which is called vernalization. Irvine notes
that this cold period also makes carrots sweeter. The best carrots,
he says, are the ones you harvest after the first frost, when the
carrots' starches develop into sugars.

While Irvine's customers are not big consumers of baby
carrots, the mildly illicit novel-like baby carrot webpage I
access through the Internet Archive Wayback Machine asserts
that the average American consumes about half their carrots
in baby form.

I also learn from Irvine and the baby carrot novel that it's a
specific type of carrot, the Imperator variety, that is used to make
baby carrots, which are in fact baby *cut* carrots. The goal is to get
four baby-cut carrots per long Imperator root, according to the
Carrot Museum. The rest of the carrot is used to make slice 'n'
dice packaged carrots or carrot juice; the very top of the carrot,
including the leaves, is used for animal feed. Imperfect carrots
and carrots that break during harvest can be repurposed as baby
carrots—which was a game changer for the carrot industry.
Developed in the early 1980s, baby carrots now comprise about
70 percent of carrot sales in the U.S. and Canada. Their popularity is instrumental in helping farmers avoid waste (though
some people argue that the better fix would be for consumers to
embrace "ugly" produce).

Imperator carrots tend to be longer and skinnier than Nantes
carrots, which are shorter and stockier, and Chantenay carrots,
which are really quite short and stubby, and Danvers carrots,
which seem to be (I haven't grown them) sort of like an American
version of Nantes with a pointed, rather than a rounded, end.

It is Elaine Spearing, who co-owns West Enderby Farm, located about an hour north of Kelowna, B.C., who clarifies for me part of the mystery of why I tasted such a difference between the carrots my grandfather grew when I was a kid and the carrots I bought in two- or five-pound bags from No Frills. Spearing and her partner are about to retire, but they've grown a lot of great carrots (including carrots they sold to Brody Irvine at Discovery Organics). One of her favourite carrots to grow is a Nantes-type hybrid called Bolero. "It's bred to be a storage carrot," she says. "If you eat it out of the ground, it's okay, but it's not as great as a summer carrot. By January, if you keep it in cool conditions, it's much nicer. It's very tasty." Another she likes to grow is also a Nantes-type, the Laguna, but that one is best eaten in warm conditions, straight from the ground.

Over an afternoon, on a video call where she takes her phone outside to show me her farm, Spearing walks me through the practicalities and economics of growing organic carrots commercially. On her farm, the soil is rich and heavy, which makes germinating and harvesting them trickier, but they grow well and taste really good. If they can't time the harvest away from a rainfall, the carrots emerge from the ground muddy or slick with a fine layer of silt. Finding success growing carrots, she says, is a matter of balancing different needs and balancing her preferences with those of the market. Some of the Nantes carrots were too brittle to harvest with a machine. An Imperator variety they once grew, called Autumn King, was nice because it had a much stronger structure. "They grew quite well, and we managed to harvest them, and we sent them to a customer, and she wasn't that impressed with them. She found them a bit hard and crunchy. She wanted that Nantes texture," Spearing tells me. Imperator carrots, in the industry, are often referred to as "cello" carrots, probably referring to the cellophane bags in which they used to be sold. They're tough. They can survive being harvested and packed with machinery. They don't shatter as easily as the Nantes.

It's probable, Spearing says, that the differences I noticed, and hold in my mind, are not simply because the No Frills carrots were crappy and the carrots my granddad grew were great—it's because they were bred and refined with different end goals in mind. My granddad's suited our purposes, using his backyard as a produce aisle in the summer. The ones from No Frills were designed to create large long roots to be mechanically harvested, to store well, to travel well, characteristics missing from my granddad's. Both sub-varieties are carrots, of course, but comparing them is a bit like comparing apples and, well, carrots.

David Catzel from FarmFolk CityFolk has been participating in a breeding program to see if they can develop an open-pollinated carrot variety that compares well to Bolero. The project is run by the Bauta Family Initiative on Canadian Seed Security; FarmFolk CityFolk is the regional partner, and David is the regional representative.

There has been so much industry support to develop hybrid varieties over the past 150 years, David says, and not nearly as much focus on open-pollinated varieties—the OP varieties have fallen behind. "Bolero is produced by one company in France," he says. "If they decide not to produce it anymore, farmers have to find a new variety."

As the regional representative for the project, David is running variety trials with twenty farmers across B.C. Farmers grow about six or seven varieties of carrots; David and his team plant the best-looking roots in isolation cages that contain pollinators in the greenhouse. Then they collect the seed, and farmers plant the carrots back out that summer. One OP variety they tried "competed with Bolero with flavour," David says, "but the yield wasn't quite there." Bolero won.

But David doesn't seem defeated. "Seeds belong in the public domain," he says. Most farmers haven't been growing seeds for generations; this project is reintroducing the idea. "Like it takes a community to raise kids, it takes a community to raise seeds."

My first-ever attempt to grow carrots was as a fall crop. I turned over a new bed, converting a patch of grass close to the house, and discovered it was part soil and part garbage fill—bits of old chicken bones, glass shards, an old aluminum can, rusty nails. I pressed onwards, seeding the new patch. What exactly happened next is lost to time and lack of experience. Did it rain too much? Was the soil too poor? Did I bury the tiny seeds too deep? Soon, bits of green began to show in the bed. Initially excited, I soon realized it was grass that had somehow survived being uprooted, turned, and buried upside down.

This year, I sowed three successions of Nantes carrots along-side some rainbow carrots leftover from the previous year, starting in early April, in a raised bed that I cultivate in the no-till style, top-dressing with compost or manure once a year in the winter. There's a mildly grizzled, happy-go-lucky small-scale farmer and vegetable gardening expert from Somerset, England, I've been watching on YouTube since we bought our house in 2019, Charles Dowding, whose advice about taproot vegetables I took to heart: "There is a growing understanding now about how soil works and how soil life works, and that we do not need to physically loosen soil in order for roots to go down and explore." In another video, Dowding constructs a six-inch-high raised bed directly on top of grass, filling it with compost and sowing carrots. This is to show,

Dowding says, that growing good carrots is possible in a fresh bed like this. Over time, I've learned to water the soil before sowing the carrots, not after, if the soil is dry; to not overseed; and to cover the seeds only very lightly with soil. If the soil is already wet and heavy, I cover the seeds with a lightweight soil mix designed for seedlings, so that they don't get weighed down or buried.

We began harvesting carrots in June and are still harvesting them in late December, as I write. Dowding's advice was correct: the vast majority have grown strong and straight and true, some deep into the part of the soil that was pretty recently grass run through with creeping buttercup.

My garden is not perfect; we haven't managed to rout out all the bindweed, a close relative of morning glory, and a bunch of acorns birds dropped into the bed over the winter began sprouting up through half a row of carrot plants as they were developing, meaning I needed to pull them and start over, as carrots do not like to be disturbed in their childhood or teenage years. But all this is normal—nothing in life is as perfect as an Instagram post, and in a home garden, even a shattered carrot, or split carrot, washed out, finds its place in your pot.

In my second year of growing carrots, I began covering my carrot rows with netting. I drive cut pieces of rebar into the edges of the beds and arch half-inch PVC pipes from one piece of rebar across the bed to another. Then I drape insect netting over top and weigh it down at the sides of the bed with large rocks. This is to prevent carrot rust flies from laying their eggs in the carrots' soil; if not prevented, the larva from the eggs burrow into the carrot roots, leaving grooves and tunnels and opening the carrot up to rot and disease. I also think it helps to retain a little bit of moisture in the soil while the seeds are germinating.

In this, my third or fourth year of growing them, I've managed to produce enough to harvest carrots weekly for over half the year—sending carrot sticks to school in my kid's lunch, making carrot-based soups, harvesting some to take down to Vancouver at Christmas, making carrot cake. Cabbage and squash, two other hearty crops I like to grow, take up a lot of sprawling, leafy space. Carrots, babied and kept moist and covered in the beginning, are afterwards quite easy and space-efficient. And now, in particular after the frost, they're as sweet and tender and crunchy as the carrots I ate so much of as a child that they began to turn my palms carotene-yellow.

HARVEST CARROT AND LENTIL SOUP

INGREDIENTS

- 2 tablespoons vegetable or olive oil
- 1 medium onion, diced
- 1 knob of ginger, two or three inches, minced
- 4 (or more) cloves of garlic
- generous bunch of carrots, peeled and chopped into large chunks
- ½ to 1 cup of split red lentils
- 2 tablespoons yellow curry paste
- vegetable stock, to cover (approx. 4 cups)
- 1 400 millilitre (13.5 fluid ounce) can of coconut milk
- salt to taste

1. Sauté the onion for five to ten minutes on medium heat.
2. Add the garlic and ginger and sauté for another minute.
3. Add the carrots and the lentils. The proportion is up to you; more carrots will mean a more carroty soup, and more lentils will mean a more lentilly soup.
4. Add the curry paste and a dash of water or stock, and mix well, until the paste is distributed.

5. Add enough vegetable stock to cover the carrots and lentils with an inch or two of liquid, probably around four cups. (You can check midway through the cooking process and add more if need be.)
6. Turn the heat up to medium-high and bring the soup to a boil, stirring occasionally.
7. Turn the heat to just above low, put the lid on the pot, and let it simmer for half an hour.
8. When the lentils are cooked and the carrots are tender, turn off the heat, take the pot off the element, and blend the soup. I do this with an immersion blender. If you're using a stand blender, skip this step for the time being.
9. Add the coconut milk. If you're using an immersion blender, blend again. If you're using a stand blender, blend now, or when the soup has cooled off enough to do so safely.

We tend to eat this soup with buttered stovetop popcorn, our soup starch of choice. While I haven't costed it out fully, I'm pretty sure, in particular because we grow the carrots and garlic, it's accidentally one of the cheapest meals we eat.

on substitution

I n late July, as I write the first draft of this essay, the garden
is entering its season of overwhelming abundance. My child,
semi-feral by this point in the summer, headed outside this morning wearing an outfit she had selected, which consisted solely of
underwear, socks, and sandals. She was heading out to play but
also to pick and eat all the berries that are ripe and ripening:
ever-bearing strawberries, blueberries, raspberries, salal.

The tomato plants are growing like weeds and bearing trusses
of fruits—but they're all still green. The snap peas, gai lan, shallots, and garlic are finished. The peppers and eggplants aren't
yet bearing; the carrots and beets and broccoli are cropping in
stages, and we're in the middle of the harvest window for the
first batch of kale, which I planted in the spring. This morning,
it's the cucumbers, green beans, and zucchini that are coming so
fast and furious we can barely keep up with eating them.

We'll eat the green beans in recipes, like salade niçoise, that
usually contain them; I'll also shoehorn them into almost everything else, using them to replace things like water chestnuts
(which I also replace with salad turnips from our CSA box) and
snap peas. They'll go into fried rice; they'll go into soup; they'll

be sautéed in butter and eaten as a side. Whatever we don't eat, I'll blanch and freeze. The cucumbers, I'll use to make a sort of dirtbag spa water—fresh slices and water refrigerated for a few hours in a large empty Adams peanut butter jar—and we'll snack on them and eat them in as many kinds of salad as possible. The zucchini, everyone but me is picky about, disliking its texture; we eat it in fritters and shredded in zucchini relish and zucchini bread. (We'll also freeze it with beans, some shredded carrot, and kale—a fried rice mix for the winter.)

I thrive in this abundance. But it was poverty and scarcity that taught me how to thrive. How to understand what each ingredient was doing in any given recipe, and how that ingredient could be swapped, lessened, or left out altogether. Because some of the most satisfying meals of my life have started with a problem: I'm missing an ingredient, or I don't eat or can't eat or can't afford an ingredient in a meal I'd like to make.

A substitution can be something simple, like crushing plain salted potato chips onto a baked mac and cheese instead of breadcrumbs, or something more complex, like using a mixture of gluten-free flours, xanthan gum, and psyllium husk gel to make gluten-free phyllo. It's understanding when it's advisable to swap carrots for squash or sweet potato and when it isn't. When an ingredient is contributing body or texture or flavour; fat or acid; what the ingredient is doing in its secondary function, if it has one—like making another key ingredient sing or adding a needed earthy note.

And that's why my definition of what makes a good cook doesn't necessarily have anything to do with how well a person can roast a lamb or sear a steak. Instead, my definition centres on how well a cook can analyze a recipe in order to adapt it—either to make a new recipe or to make a similar one with whatever ingredients are presently available.

"We can't deny the parallels our current COVID-19 pandemic shares with the Great Depression," baker B. Dylan Hollis told Food52 in 2021. "Many of us are still stuck inside, money is short, and the hindrances to eating out in public has forced us to return to our kitchens and reflect on it as a place to create and sustain us more than ever before. Baking historical recipes is one of the most interesting and engaging ways to experience the past, and through that: understand our place in the present time."

Hollis had recently baked a water pie on TikTok. The recipe, which requires a pie crust, water, sugar, flour, vanilla extract, and butter, was one of several Depression-era recipes that made the rounds during the first year and a half of COVID, before most public health agencies across North America shrugged their shoulders and declared the pandemic over, and everything went "back to normal."

People also made peanut butter bread, compost soup, dandelion salad, and sourdough bread; they spoke with their grandparents and turned to the past for advice about how to avoid food waste and eat cheaply. There was a huge bump in vegetable gardening, harkening back to Second World War era victory gardens. People bought so much seed that some companies faced shortages. Others, such as West Coast Seeds, couldn't package seeds fast enough to keep up with demand, even though they'd doubled their production capacity by 2021. Though most articles at the time focused on seeds, supply outpaced demand in everything related to home gardening. Getting your hands on good, decently priced manure or compost, for example, was cutthroat, a whisper network of access to the excrement of cows and horses and alpacas.

In 2022, this fervour tapered off. "This past year, we have experienced a much greater stability with gardeners and growers returning to normal buying patterns, creating a very welcome plateau," Elizabeth Clark, marketing manager at West Coast Seeds, told me by email. While some new gardeners have continued with the practice they picked up over the pandemic, others went back to doing what they had been doing before. Which makes sense: vegetable gardening takes quite a bit of patience, time, and planning. As does cooking. It's unreasonable to expect individuals to undo the industrialization of food production as they work at least forty hours a week, commute, and act as caregivers for kids or friends or loved ones; everyone is pretty busy just trying to keep their bills paid. But Clark did also tell me that demand remains strong and that many people have continued to "grow food from seed as part of an environmentally sustainable and food secure lifestyle." And of course, this resonates with me. But as inflation presses food budgets, and there are no more government income programs to blunt the economic impacts of the pandemic, and social assistance rates haven't kept up for decades, it's food bank use that has increased the most, much more than vegetable gardening.

When the pandemic hit, I was already gardening and cooking a lot, and I'd spent enough time making what are now called "struggle meals" when I was penniless and hungry that I had no real desire to look back to Depression-era recipes. I did start baking a lot more, though, and putting time into making more elaborate food. I bought an apple-green stand mixer when it went on sale for half off and finally—why didn't I sooner?—a digital thermometer. I learned how to make ice cream and gluten-free rough puff pastry and Swiss meringue buttercream. Craving baklava, I made my own phyllo. But it wasn't until I listened to Samin Nosrat, author of *Salt, Fat, Acid, Heat*, talk about food on her limited-run podcast *Home Cooking* that I realized how much I'd actually picked up, over the years, about food and cooking—more than I realized I knew, and for the most part, it had nothing to do with my more recent ability to make a perfect crème caramel.

Part of what Nosrat does on *Home Cooking* is to suggest meal options from a broad spread of cultural traditions, based on what people have lurking in their fridges, freezers, and pantries— alongside ways to stock fridges, freezers, and pantries that will give home cooks the ability to create variety in their meals. Because of this, Nosrat rarely offers a straight recipe.

In the inaugural episode, for example, she offers approaches to making cheesy scrambled eggs, pea soup, split pea dal, lentil rice with fried raisins, a quick-pickled beet and lentil salad. The pea soup is made using frozen English peas and whatever herbs you have access to. After you start eating from your pantry and freezer for a time, Nosrat says, the number one thing you'll begin to crave is freshness. And that's what this soup offers.

"For people who've been wanting to become better cooks, this is the opportunity that everyone's been waiting for because what makes you a better cook is practice," Nosrat says near the top of the show. "It's all of that experimentation, and how do I combine these things? And those are the things that we will save in our culinary filing cabinets of the mind and which will help us for the rest of our lives."

When I had no money and was cobbling together meals, my body instinctively craved the basics, foods that would keep me fuelled and ward off scurvy and anemia. But Nosrat is right about what happens when you survive on grains and pulses—it is the pop of sweetness from adding frozen corn or peas, the zing from grated ginger, the freshness of mint or parsley or cilantro, the dollop of sour cream, that makes it possible to eat in again rather than running up your credit card in search of novelty.

Cooking with what I have lying around is different for me now that I am middle class. It took me a long time to become middle class, well into my thirties, and when I did, I turned into my grandparents: well-stocked pantry, well-stocked freezer, savings account growing very slowly every month, except for the months I need to go to the dentist or send money to the farm in order to buy my CSA for the year.

The main difference, like Nosrat's buffet of recipes suggests, is that my pantry allows me to pivot into different countries or regions of cuisine on a whim—everything from Dijon mustard and mustard seeds to honey and maple syrup and many kinds of vinegars; soy sauce and sesame oil and Lao Gan Ma chili sauce and gochujang. Pine nuts and sesame seeds, almonds and peanuts and pistachios. Rice noodles, gluten-free pasta, gnocchi, cornmeal, short-grain and long-grain rice, wild rice, popcorn kernels, buckwheat groats. Red lentils, French lentils, black-eyed peas, pinto beans, scarlet runners, black beans, small white baby limas. Chickpeas I buy in cans—the aquafaba's useful as an egg substitute. Baked beans. Frozen peas and corn. Frozen blueberries. Roasted seaweed sheets, and furikake seasoning, which, in my household, we call "the shaky seaweed."

I know the landscape of the cupboards like a park ranger knows their home park. I am thinking ahead four or five days at any given time, planning out how and when the perishables will need to be used, what I'm craving, what my kid likes, what we haven't had in a while, what will need to be prepped the night before. If we want to eat a galette and salad on a weeknight, I'll need to make the dough and prep the innards the night before. If I'll be cooking beans in the slow cooker, I'll place it on the counter the night before, filling it with the dry ingredients to make life easier in the morning.

This flexibility makes it possible to eat beans every night of the week and not get tired of them. If one night is pinto beans and rice with fermented hot sauce and sour cream, the next can be a black-eyed pea stew over polenta, and the night after that, chickpeas and roasted broccoli with peanut sauce and rice noodles. One night, lentil loaf; the next, warm lentil salad dressed in brown butter vinaigrette.

If you asked me to define wealth, it would be housing security and this. I have three batches of homemade ice cream in my freezer right now. If I want rosemary for my roast potatoes, I can pick it fresh outside. Once a year, in the fall, I get to harvest from my saffron crocuses and make a pot of golden rice. What more could I ever want in life?

A 2019 essay by Alison Herman for *The Ringer* goes into what makes the *New York Times*' Cooking comment section so good, when so many other recipe comment sections are so terrible. The essay opens with Daniel Lavery lampooning said terrible comment sections: "I didn't have any eggs, so I replaced them with a banana-chia-flaxseed pulse. It turned out terrible; this recipe is terrible." The wrong kind of substitution.

But, Herman continues, *NYT* Cooking's comments—or "notes," as editor Sam Sifton calls them—are different. "Cooking's are genuinely additive, have a ready-made takeaway, and best of all, inspire downright bonhomie toward my fellow man," Herman writes.

Cooking's notes, unlike so many others, offer hints, explication, tips, and good substitutions. They send some of Herman's interviewees so far into the weeds that the essay briefly turns to what a recipe even is. ("Everything is a derivative of something else," Sifton says.) They're moderated; notes that don't contribute much of value are rejected, never seeing the oven light of day.

Freed from the stricture of the page, loosed into the free-wheeling conversational style of the podcast, Nosrat's *Home Cooking* recipes are similar. They become a verbal diagram for how to interpret the idea of a meal that will end up looking a little bit different for everyone. She offers the reasoning behind certain treatments of food—things that will help the dish become crunchy or properly seasoned or melt-in-your-mouth—but her approach also places a lot of trust in her listeners.

This same approach features in Nosrat's foundational book *Salt, Fat, Acid, Heat*, which she began writing about a year into interning at Chez Panisse. "Salt, fat, acid, and heat were the four elements that guided basic decision making in every single dish, no matter what," she writes in the introduction. This is the structure through which Nosrat understands cooking and disseminates her knowledge about it, and it pervades the book as she explains why and how she does what she does.

Nosrat's epiphany occurs after she's been cooking and learning at Chez Panisse for a while, and she begins to recognize patterns in the treatment of cuts of meat and delicate fish fillets and deep-fried foods and seasoning as the restaurant's menu changes daily. Theory and praxis.

What's more complicated is creating the space and opportunity to learn—Chez Panisse, I'm guessing, has limited internship spots. Food security programs that feed kids and bring cooks and farmers into classes can help, and they're experiencing revivals in some areas of the country. Practice, including learning alongside friends or family members, and access to recipes like Nosrat's that sidle into technical territory can also help home cooks improve their improvisational skills. (Alton Brown's recipes and TV shows, the *Bon Appétit* Test Kitchen, and *Serious Eats* are three more resources that explain the why and how of ingredients—making it possible to better understand how to substitute them and when not to.) These are the kinds of recipes I consult to learn how to make and improve upon everything from pâte à choux to pastry cream to onion rings. Because the more we're able to learn about the underlying science and theories of cooking and baking, the more we're able to adapt any given recipe based on what we have in our gardens and pantries. To make good substitutions instead of terrible ones.

"Fancy is overrated," Nosrat says near the end of *Home Cooking*'s first episode to guest Josh Malina, who has just gone into some detail describing his latke recipe and then much less detail describing some Instant Pot black beans mixed with a tomato-cilantro slurry, before adding the caveat that he's more of a hearty staples type of cook than a fancy type of cook.

What isn't overrated is using what you have to make satisfying food and then sharing it with others. What isn't overrated is understanding what will ring the bells of your cravings, or how to adapt a food you love for a friend with allergies, or who's vegan, and coming over for dinner.

When a meal or an ingredient is unfamiliar, a recipe offers a way into something new. As it becomes more familiar, it becomes possible to see its structure and what you may swap out for something else. It's this part that is the beating heart of any recipe worth its salt. And it's this familiarity, and understanding, I've been working towards my entire cooking life.

There's nothing wrong with enjoying what's fancy. But it's also freeing to dispense with fancy in favour of what's personally satisfying, what's available, what's right for you—to treat cooking and baking like a lifelong pursuit of alchemy, with the goal of making the sum ever better than its parts.

KALE PESTO: AN ODE TO SUBSTITUTION

Traditional pesto, or pesto alla Genovese, is made from basil, garlic, pine nuts, Parmigiano-Reggiano, olive oil, and salt, ideally in a mortar and pestle. ("Pestle" and "pesto" share the same word origins.)

Before I had a garden, I didn't quite understand why anyone would eat anything other than the classic—basil is one of the world's best flavours. After I had a garden, I got it: kale has an unbeatably long growing window, and as long as your soil is half-decent, it basically grows itself. It's available at times of the year in Canada when almost nothing else survives outdoors.

This pesto is a highly substitutable recipe. A looser definition of pesto also allows you to use up an overabundance of chard, garlic scapes, carrot tops, lovage, or even softer greens like spinach and mizuna. If you don't have a garden, you can even forage stinging nettles, which emerge in the spring, until they begin to flower. (I recommend wearing gloves to protect your hands and researching foraging tips in order to harvest responsibly.)

When I make kale pesto, I tend to use walnuts, as they're much cheaper than pine nuts and pair well with kale. If you're using different greens, you'll want to think about which nuts pair best with their flavour profiles—spinach goes well with almonds, for example, and carrot tops go best with walnuts or pecans.

INGREDIENTS

- 1 large bunch greens: kale, chard, stinging nettles, garlic scapes, or carrot tops
- 1/2 cup raw nuts or seeds, such as walnuts, pepitas, almonds, or pistachios
- ½ cup olive oil
- 2 cloves garlic

- fistful of grated Parmigiano-Reggiano
- pinch of salt
- a few generous dashes of pepper
- squeeze of lemon (optional)

1. Toast the nuts in a dry cast iron pan, just until you can begin to smell their toasty aroma. Take off the heat and set aside while you prepare the greens.
2. Wash and dry the greens thoroughly and prepare them. For kale and chard, remove the spine from each leaf. Carrot tops are good to go after washing. For stinging nettles, wear gloves and remove the leaves carefully from the spiky spine and cook them briefly in boiling water. (For garlic scape pesto, omit the garlic from the recipe, remove the area that would become the garlic flower on the scape, and chop the rest roughly before blending.)
3. Roughly chop the greens and set aside.
4. Add the toasted nuts, garlic, and Parmigiano-Reggiano to a food processor; pulse until the nuts and garlic are fairly well chopped.
5. Add the greens. With the food processor running on low, drizzle in the olive oil until you have a relatively smooth paste. It's okay if it's a little chunky, and the greens have a bit of texture.
6. Add pepper and salt to taste. Add a squeeze of lemon to brighten the flavour and counteract any bitterness.

the garden will bloom again

The first seed to break the surface of the soil in 2021 was celery. Next came the bergamot and lemongrass, and then, more slowly, the leeks. Their greens were tiny pinpricks against the deep brown and perlite white of the potting soil; under the bright grow light in my kitchen, they began to unfurl, stretch upward. It was early March of my third year in my house, with my garden.

Outside, there was a large pile of horse manure sitting on our driveway, which is separated from the backyard portion of the garden by a deer fence, the cheapest deer fence we could construct, made out of six-foot metal fencing lashed onto eight-foot metal T-posts that we drove into the ground using large rocks—rocks the size of a very generous sourdough loaf. To do this, I wore Will's bike helmet and braced the T-posts with my hands; Will stood above me on a ladder, whacking the posts as hard and as evenly as he could. We must have looked odd to our neighbours. But at least one rock cleaved apart from the pressure of repeated whacking, bonking the helmet and rolling off its side onto the ground.

We live on a quarter acre with a view of the Pacific Ocean, in a microclimate that is a little warmer than much of the surrounding area, warm enough that tomatoes grow vigorously outdoors. But not warm enough for peppers or eggplant. The backyard is set up in beds separated by wood-chip paths, with a few six-inch-high raised beds and one foot-high raised bed. Will and I share the beds. About a third are nursery beds for the trees and shrubs he propagates, and two-thirds are for vegetables. We build archways for the squash, melons, cucumbers, and beans out of laurels and string or leftover fencing. A small patch of grass remains in the northwest corner, large enough to hold our picnic table and the little wading pool we set up in the summer. There is an asparagus patch and an herb garden, a cherry tree and two apple trees, a number of shrubs that bear currants and blueberries, and a strawberry patch. Our hoop house and our greenhouse.

The front yard, which came with a giant blue spruce, is where Will's trees and shrubs go when they are mature enough to suit his vision for the yard—into organically shaped beds that work with the slight grade and the shape of the space. There is no deer fence in the front yard, so the most vulnerable plants, like the ginkgo biloba we splurged on from a nursery on the island, are ringed by little cylinders of metal fencing or, in the case of a small spotted laurel, nestled underneath an overturned bird cage that showed up at the curb in front of a neighbour's house one garbage day.

We live in the house in almost the exact haphazard state that we bought it in—but the garden, we've transformed. Are still transforming.

One of our earliest spring tasks every year is to spread manure or compost, wheelbarrow by wheelbarrow, over the garden beds. This is a task that Sinclair, now six, has helped with ever since she could walk. In 2020, when she was two years old, she used a small plastic spade. By 2021, she was using her own real little shovel, which she'd received as a present from a friend.

The first spring of COVID, Sinclair and I were digging out sod together in the backyard to make new beds for trailing squash. I was listening to the news every day. There were pictures of cooling trucks parked behind New York City hospital morgues. Li Wenliang, a whistleblower who had noticed the emergence of what he identified as a new SARS-like virus and alerted other doctors, had died after contracting COVID himself. People were sheltering in their apartments. Everyone was talking about essential work. The docuseries *Lenox Hill* aired a special pandemic episode, taking viewers inside the hospital as health care workers struggled to keep up with the intense pace and requirements of caring for COVID patients—crying, their post-shift faces reddened and grooved with lines from pandemic PPE.

On the northern Sunshine Coast, distant from the initial main epicentres of the pandemic, we focused on growing the garden. As she shovelled, Sinclair wrapped her two-year-old mouth around the word "coronavirus," repeating it over and over as we worked in crisp air and sunshine.

That spring, the sprouts and blooms emerged two by two with worsening news and our worsening anxiety. But the garden provided hope. A literally grounded vision of the future. We built raised beds from cedar planks, spread mushroom manure, planted our first snap peas. Hellebore and heather blooms offered colour against the grey early spring sky; blueberry blossoms were followed by blueberries; tiny broccoli seedlings were followed by leaves and the eruption of edible florets. Everything in the garden felt meaningful, full of life.

The second pandemic spring was different. Alongside a vanishing wick of hope, our early preparatory time in the garden unearthed the difficulties of the previous year. My nana had died, and I hadn't gone home to attend her funeral. I felt unable to mourn, as if I'd hit a pause button on life, one the continuous seasonal rhythms of the garden wasn't quite unsticking. It still felt good to be outside, working on spring tasks, but the meaning felt different—tinged with sadness and frustration and nihilism.

I wasn't alone in this. When Lori Weidenhammer, the author of *Victory Gardens for Bees*, was a child in Saskatchewan, she spent the winters looking at seed catalogues and thinking about what she'd grow the following season. In Vancouver, where she lives now, there's an idiom that marks the beginning of the season for her: "When the forsythia is blooming, it's time to prune the roses."

But the events of 2020 complicated her relationship to the hopefulness of spring gardening in 2021. "Yesterday I was exercising outdoors by this currant bush, that last year at this time of the year I was exercising at, and it was just the beginning of the lockdown, so it triggered all of these horrible, horrible feelings," she told me.

The third and fourth pandemic springs brought their own lessons. As I spend more concentrated time on the farming and gardening and homesteading sides of Instagram—I am always looking to learn and grow in spring—the algorithm starts serving me content from preppers and people who do not believe in pasteurizing milk but do believe in water-bath canning it. People who mistrust the government about vaccines and digital banking and, apparently, botulism. It's depressing, makes my stomach churn with anxiety.

Meanwhile, in 2023, drought persists. Cedars in my neighbourhood are turning brown and dying off. The wildfire haze settles in early. We water half the garden diligently, but with a sprinkler, so we can keep up with its needs. For the other half of the garden, I use last year's drip line from a local farm to set up irrigation for my tomatoes, squash, melons, cucumbers, and celery. My friend Jen helps me plan and figure out the hardware I need to buy to complete the system; we order some online and get some at the local Rona, and Will does one final trip to Pete's Plumbing for some PVC pipe we'll use as a header tube.

Often, I feel as if I'm floating above my body. Still, the rhythms of attending to the garden's needs bring me back into myself for a moment as I turn on the spigot to start the morning watering or enact a gentle, measured yank to harvest a pea or behead a chamomile flower.

Spring reminds me that life is cyclical, rather than linear— or perhaps that it's both cyclical *and* linear. Some years the potential the season symbolizes is easy, clean; other years it's bittersweet, a hope that emerges despite, rather than because of, its surroundings.

The winter and early spring provide natural moments to pause and reflect for gardeners. In their essay "Winter Is for Regeneration. The Garden's—and Yours, Too," 'Cúagilákv (Jess Háusti) writes about the connection between trauma, mental health, grief, and gardening.

For 'Cúagilákv, the link between gardening and mental health was solidified when they transformed an empty lot into a community garden the year following the Nathan E. Stewart oil spill, which polluted what had been until then the breadbasket of Heiltsuk territory, impacting "dozens of marine and intertidal species that hundreds of Heiltsuk families relied on for sustenance." 'Cúagilákv had been the incident commander during the spill; when the acute response phase ended, they struggled to rediscover the pace of daily life and were eventually diagnosed with post-traumatic stress disorder.

"We knew that growing carrots and onions could never replace the tainted clam beds or the plethora of ocean relatives that were poisoned by the spill," 'Cúagilákv writes. "But it gave me a small sense of stability, control and agency over my family's food security—enough to help pull me through the worst of the mental and spiritual anguish. And I hope it gave that gift to others too."

In the winter, they write, "The deeper work that supports our seasonal thriving is still creating magic in our raised beds; beneath the frost, the layers of kelp mulch and decaying bracken fern, the soil is rebuilding itself with deep inhales of cold winter air."

Rest in winter and early spring is purposeful, active in a way that contrasts with the heady midsummer time of abundant harvest—but it is key to that time of abundance. It is an act of hope and care to tend to the soil and participate in the ecosystem and ready it for the coming year.

But part of what offers hope contains sadness for me: the garden will bloom again, but not everyone and everything will be here to see it. The return of last year's rhythms, the return of tiny pinpricks of green against the rich and joyous brown of the earth—they hold promise for the future, but they also remind me of what we have lost.

Maybe, though, this is also part of gardening's gift, offering a way into the grief I have not been able to process, the stress I thought was going to be acute but has instead become chronic, the anger I have that the early pandemic hope of social cohesion in crisis gave way to the same pressures of capitalism and conspiracy that have been making life feel more and more unlivable.

It makes sense that spreading manure, or compost, is the act that drums up everything I've been processing over the winter—composting being an act that embraces death and transformation, turning organic matter into material that will feed the soil. The sound of my shovel against the metal of the wheelbarrow, the way it catches on the rivets when it's getting empty, the way the garden beds look when they've been top-dressed, deep brown and ready for the coming year—everything so familiar, sweaty, and meditative, and of course it doesn't engender the same feelings it did last year, or the year before that, because I'm a different person, needing to learn different lessons.

I remember the years best by their springs—the way they unearth the past and offer a generative way forward into the cacophony of summer. I also look forward to them most, even though they're not always easy. They hold change and complexity, the promise of harvest. A reminder that the garden holds the breadth and depth of emotional seasons, and so can we.

a fifty-pound bag of potatoes

On the eve of my third year at university, my mother made one of the only trips she'd ever make to visit me in the seven years I spent living half an hour down the road from her in Guelph. She brought her boyfriend. Together, they bought a fifty-pound bag of potatoes. He worked in produce, and they'd been on sale.

It was summer, and I was then living in the two-bedroom apartment above the curry restaurant downtown where me, my then-partner, and my roommate all worked. Our kitchen was on the east side of the apartment, with a window that opened out onto a peaked roof we sometimes climbed onto to smoke a joint. Our rent was $267 each, but we were still chronically broke—money like water we had no container for.

If you've never carried a fifty-pound bag of potatoes: the best way to do it is over a shoulder, distributing the weight evenly. You can also opt for a fireman's carry, slinging it over both shoulders and keeping it in place with your arms. It feels eerily like a lumpy torso.

If you're strong, the most annoying thing about it is the lumps. If you're not very strong, your knees might buckle. If you're somewhere in the middle, you'll be able to carry it, but your whole being will be focussed on carrying it, unable to think or hope or desire anything else.

My mother and her boyfriend had been drinking at a bar next to his produce shop one evening before I left home, when I still worked at his produce store, when I was tasked to bring a fifty-pound bag of potatoes over to the caterer who worked out of the bar's kitchen. I hefted it onto my shoulders and carried it down a short set of stairs at the front of the store, then across the parking lot towards the bar.

My parents were still married at the time and were not really supposed to have other significant others; I was thinking about this as I hefted the potatoes down a second set of stairs into the bar, wondering what I was about to see—a hand where it shouldn't be, knees touching underneath the table of a booth. I hadn't anticipated any other surprises, but as I was carrying the potatoes through the bar, a man approached me. He told me he'd help me, I said it wasn't necessary, and then he took advantage of the fact that I was occupied with the potatoes to, in the guise of "helping," grope my teenage body.

After I came unfrozen, I yelled at him and beelined for the kitchen. My mother followed. She told me I misunderstood the man's intentions and needed to apologize. My mouth began to feel salty, as if I was going to throw up. My face got hot; my cheeks turned red. It was a dizzying anger, a new level of betrayal. I left out a door I'd never used before and found myself in the bar's overflow parking lot, looking at a Second World War fighter plane mounted on a pole. My mother didn't follow; she went back to her boyfriend and her glass of white wine.

Gifts from my mother so often came with strings attached. But I think this one was really from her boyfriend. I'm sure she wasn't thinking about the incident with the man in the bar when they dropped the potatoes off. I don't even think they stuck around for lunch. I was grateful for the free food, even though I did immediately flash back to being groped and getting in trouble for objecting to being groped. The potatoes carried a psychic weight as well as the gift of calories.

It also felt like a challenge had been issued: how were three people in a hot second-floor walk-up going to get through them before they began to rot? Would the memory of the man who'd assaulted me wither and shrink along with the contents of the bag?

Different varieties of potatoes have different ideal uses. Waxy varieties, like new potatoes (or baby potatoes of any variety) and fingerlings and Norland potatoes, are best in recipes where you want the potato to stay together, solid—in salade niçoise, in a stew or chunk soup. Medium-starch potatoes, like Yukon Golds and Kennebec, are best for scalloped potatoes, potatoes au gratin, and mayonnaise-based potato salad, where you want the potato to retain a bit of its shape while allowing its cooked exterior to mix with the dairy or mayo to make a creamy, starchy sauce. Starchy potatoes, like russets, are best for making French fries and for baking; once baked, they can be added to a creamy soup. Either medium starchy or starchy can make good mashed potatoes; Alton Brown suggests using a two-to-one ratio of starchy to waxed, but it comes down to preference.

Starchy potatoes become gluey if you overmix them, which is why cooks recommend using a potato ricer, which reduces a potato uniformly, and with one press, into a workable base for salt and butter and milk and sour cream. If you don't mind—or if you, like me, prefer—mashed potatoes with some lumps and texture, a masher works fine. For a puréed soup like a cheesy potato and broccoli, bake or boil the potato separately and add it to your soup *after* you've puréed the stock and aromatics and broccoli—blenders also make potatoes gluey. (On *Good Eats*, Brown suggests adding a slurry of riced baked potato and dairy to soup to achieve a perfect creamy consistency.)

When we received the fifty pounds of potatoes, we did not bother ourselves with what kind of potatoes they were. (They were probably russets.) We ate them mashed, we ate them roasted, we ate them in curry, we ate them in potato salad, we ate them with scrambled eggs, we ate them sliced thin at the bottom of a frittata. Eating so many of them made me think glancingly of the potato famine, made me wonder if there was something familial or ancestral about craving the potato as a warm, filling starch.

One day when I was hungry and rooting around the cupboard for something I could pair with potatoes, I remembered the shepherd's pie we ate growing up. My mother made it with ground beef, so it was technically a cottage pie. She never topped it with grated cheese—just dragged a fork across the surface to make ridges. I figured I could make something similar and vegetarian.

The first time I made it, I used texturized vegetable protein—better known as TVP, bland shelf-stable flakes patented in the 1960s amidst concerns the world was facing an imminent shortage of animal protein; it was abandoned to dusty hippie stores selling carob soon after the shortage failed to hit—and onions, garlic, vegetables, and stock. It was fine but lacked something. I wanted to go to bed satisfied, with a warm and full stomach. The next time I made it, I was stoned and noticed a tin of baked beans on the shelf. The beans would add some protein and fibre, and their tomato sauce would mix well with the vegetables and a smaller amount of TVP, thickening the sauce. It worked.

Another recipe I soon began making, which, much like the vegetarian shepherd's pie, can also be treated as a repository for whatever vegetables you have on hand, was a lentil loaf I could have sworn was adapted from the classic '70s vegetarian cookbook *Laurel's Kitchen*—but now that I've checked both it and my *Moosewood Cookbook*, which has a lentil walnut burger but no lentil loaf, I'm at a loss as to its provenance. If I found it online, I found it online at the height of the popularity of *Homestar Runner*.

The lentil loaf is better than meatloaf; you can serve it with a simple leafy salad dressed with a Dijon vinaigrette, but it's really best served with mashed potatoes and mushroom gravy. If you use oil instead of butter to cook your vegetables, it's also vegan.

I'd place both of these meals in the realm of American vegetarian cooking that has its roots in the '70s, intentional communities, and back-to-the-land-ing. When I was adapting the shepherd's pie I'd eaten as a child, what I reached for was something I could swap vegetarian proteins into; this is something, if you have eaten at enough vegan and vegetarian restaurants run by white hippies, you'll notice everywhere. Tofu marinated and used in sandwiches; ingredients that are rightly cornerstones of a particular cuisine plucked ahistorically from their usual contexts and harnessed for their saltiness or their spice or their umami or their ability to substitute for meat.

A few of my other cornerstone recipes, like marinated breaded tofu (eaten on Thanksgiving or Christmas as a turkey substitute) or balsamic-glazed tofu (eaten with mashed potatoes and salad or on a sandwich with avocado, cucumber, sprouts, and mayo), commit the same sins, using tofu as a blank canvas instead of an ingredient with a rich history.

This wasn't something I was thinking about when I reached for baked beans (British!) to throw into a quintessentially British meal. But it might have been part of the reason the recipe worked out.

Then again, though potatoes are now a cornerstone of American and European cuisines, they're originally from Peru, where they were cultivated in the Andes and used in Andean cuisines—boiled and mashed and fried, but also fermented and frozen and preserved. It was Spanish colonizers who brought them back to Europe; initially, Europeans were wary of them, the story goes, because Europeans were a poisoning people, and potatoes are part of the nightshade family. (Potatoes contain glycoalkaloids; the leaves and flowers of the plant should be avoided, as should any sprouts or skin that's turned green from exposure to light.) Because they're easy to cultivate and produce good harvests, when they did finally take off, they were seen as peasant food—sustenance for labourers.

And that's mostly why I've eaten them: they're cheaper than bread and just as hearty. Growing up, on special occasions, it wasn't uncommon to see them three ways—roasted, mashed, scalloped—at a larger family meal.

Even now, a go-to quick and inexpensive dinner at my house often includes potatoes. When we're stuck and low on groceries, it's usually roasted potatoes, maybe with the addition of other root vegetables—sweet potatoes, carrots, beets—and an egg scramble, always with cheese and often with greens, or scapes or peppers when they're in season. In the winter, we eat them mashed and in stews and casseroles; in the summer, in potato salad, in a cheesy broccoli soup made almost entirely from ingredients harvested from the yard.

Back in Guelph, when I was still trying to figure out how I was going to survive my early twenties, when I would wake up sometimes having no understanding of how my apartment had gotten into the state it had gotten into, when I was still very actively angry at my mother, and equally quite scared of her, we had the fifty-pound bag of potatoes to get through.

Though the apartment was overly warm, and we all had access to staff meals and were all dirtbags, we managed to eat through basically all of the potatoes, until, at the bottom of the bag, they finally began to go soft and sprout. The funniest thing was that in our months-long rush to eat through the fifty-pound bag, we entirely neglected a much smaller half-eaten plastic sack of potatoes one of us, probably me, had dragged home from the No Frills in a backpack and placed in a cupboard.

After the large bag was finished and removed, the apartment smelled very curiously of rotten potatoes, which is one of the worst smells in the world. The fifty-pound bag—which did remind me less and less of the time the man groped me as it shrunk—had haunted us for the duration of its presence; it seemed like it would *continue* to haunt us after we were gone.

That is, until I found the real culprits, which had been reduced to a gooey, maggot-filled mess in their forgotten plastic bag. It was a mess I begged my roommate to deal with; we put plastic bags over his hands and doubled up a few more to use as a garbage bag to ensure the offending sack didn't drip rotten potato juice as we took it down to the dumpster.

If you think any of this dissuaded us from immediately eating more potatoes, you'd be wrong. My favourite staff meal at the curry restaurant was cardamom-and-cinnamon-scented rice with chana and aloo gobi. In other words, a chickpea-based curry, and a cauliflower and potato one. It's highly likely I gagged about the rotten potatoes one overly bright morning and was immediately back to eating them later that night while microwaving other people's curries and prepping raita and brushing garlic butter over naans.

And I've continued to make variations of the vegetarian shepherd's pie and the lentil loaf since the fifty-pound bag of potatoes entered my life. I developed the recipe for the shepherd's pie only a few years after the time I attempted to run chocolate milk through a coffee maker seeking a shortcut to a mocha. (Do not do this; the chocolate milk is too thick to make its way through the coffee filter, so it bubbles up and over the sides instead.) Unlike many of my other earlier creations, the shepherd's pie stuck.

If I could go back in time and give my younger self one recipe to make a couple times as a celebratory meal with our excess of potatoes, it would be a pommes dauphine I ate during the pandemic with my partner at a bistro-style French restaurant in Kitsilano, while our kid was having a sleepover with her cousin. They came alongside steak dressed in butter, and I was expecting them to be pommes dauphinoise, because I'd misread the menu. They were absolutely not gluten-free, but I didn't realize that until later when my stomach hurt. All I knew at the time was that I'd accidentally ordered some kind of strange French tater tot that arrived to the table perfectly fluffy and deep-fried, the jus from the steak acting as a perfect kind of dipping gravy.

The ingredients to make it—(gluten-free) flour, eggs, milk, butter, salt and pepper, potatoes—aren't any more complicated than anything I cooked with in my twenties. But the process is complex, like some of the Peruvian processes for turning potatoes into otherworldly things with pleasantly confounding textures—only unmistakably French, because it involves combining choux pastry with mashed potatoes and then deep-frying them.

When I make them at home, I study a few different recipes and then settle on a *Serious Eats* version; this way, as long as I am looking for the same end product they're looking for (crisp outside, light and fluffy inside), someone has done the recipe testing for me, and I do not need to futz around with my choux and potato ratios.

I begin the day before by removing a small Tupperware full of vegetable demi-glace from the deep freeze and thawing it in the fridge. On the day of, I first start the gravy, sautéing onion from the grocery store with some frozen leeks I grew last year. Once the gravy is bubbling away, I turn it to low and make my choux. Then I begin boiling a pound of russet potatoes, making a salad with mizuna and cilantro from the yard, and a simple vinaigrette, while they cook. I rice the potatoes using an antique ricer I got off Facebook from a woman who trawls the local thrift stores and estate sales and then upsells, tacking on a small finder's fee. I heat canola oil in a Dutch oven, which I got on sale from Canadian Tire, until it reaches 340 degrees, and then I use two spoons to drop slightly wonky balls of dough into the hot oil, ten per batch. While I'm frying, I make some maple-balsamic-glazed tofu. All in all, it takes about two hours, and we have a fancy vegetarian Sunday dinner. These pommes dauphine are lighter, airer than the ones I had in Vancouver; they go so well with the deep umami of the leek and onion gravy, with the light and slightly acidic crunch of the salad on the side. The recipe says it's meant to feed four to six, but the three of us polish it off. Sinclair eats four helpings, dipping her potatoes in a ramekin of gravy and, when she's done, drinking the gravy straight up.

Is it strange that my favourite gift from my mother is a fifty-pound bag of potatoes that reminded me of being assaulted in her presence? Probably. But I think it's attributable to the enduring nourishment and culinary power of the potato. Potatoes could remind me of sexual assault, of the enduring anger I feel towards my mother, and of poverty, but they don't, usually. On a daily basis, they're simply a reliable, flexible cornerstone. They are so good at adapting to their surroundings, becoming crispy or crunchy, soft and fluffy, even gluey.

They are so transmutable that when Sinclair turned four, I began to call her my little sack of potatoes (pronounced puh-tatt-ohs). She weighed just under forty pounds, and it was no longer an effortless task to heft her up and carry her. So I began to say, "Oof, my little sack of potatoes, you're getting so strong!" and then carried her wherever she wanted to go, until I tired of it or she did. Sometimes, still, we gallop along and I pretend to be a horse, bouncing her and making cluh-clop, cluh-clop, cluh-clop noises with my tongue.

VEGETARIAN SHEPHERD'S PIE

This recipe can be made more simply and adapted to suit your needs. Can't afford celery or sour cream? Omit them. Have some snap peas or some sad-looking broccoli in the fridge? Add it.

INGREDIENTS

- 2 tablespoons vegetable or olive oil
- 1 medium-sized onion, diced
- 2 ribs of celery, diced
- 1 large carrot, diced
- 4 cloves of garlic (at least), minced
- 1 398 millilitre (14 fluid ounce) can of tomato-based baked beans

- large handful of texturized vegetable protein (TVP)
- 1/2 cup of vegetable stock (or 1 teaspoon of soy sauce and 1/2 cup of water)
- 1 1/2 tablespoons herbes de Provence
- 1/2 cup frozen peas
- 1/2 cup frozen corn
- 5 large or 8 medium-sized potatoes
- 2 tablespoons butter
- 2 tablespoons sour cream
- splash of milk
- salt and pepper

1. Preheat your oven to 375°F (190°C). Heat oil in a saucepan (or, if you have it, a cast iron Dutch oven— you'll be able to put the mash on top and throw the whole thing into the oven). Add onion, celery, and carrot, and allow it to cook for about five minutes before adding the garlic.
2. Meanwhile, set a large salted pot of water boiling. Peel the potatoes and chop them into large cubes. Drop the potatoes into the boiling water and let them cook until fork tender—about 15 minutes.
3. To your onions, celery, carrot, and garlic, add your baked beans, TVP, herbes de Provence, and stock. Once the mixture begins to bubble, turn it down to low and let it hang out until your potatoes are cooked.
4. When your potatoes are ready, mix the frozen corn and peas into the shepherd's pie base. If you've been working in a non-oven-safe saucepan, transfer the mixture to an oven-safe casserole dish.
5. Make the mashed potatoes: drain the water; rice the potatoes or use a masher; add butter, sour cream, splash of milk, and salt and pepper; and mix.

6. Dollop the mashed potatoes onto the shepherd's pie base. Spread them out with a spoon or spatula so everything is evenly covered. Drag a fork across the mash in rows to create a series of parallel lines.
7. Place in the preheated oven and cook at 375°F for 30 minutes. The peaks of the mash should get a little browned and crispy, and the shepherd's pie base should bubble up the sides of the dish.

LENTIL LOAF

INGREDIENTS

- butter or oil for sautéing
- 1 large carrot, diced
- 1 medium-sized onion, diced
- 2 ribs celery, diced
- 3 to 5 cloves of garlic, minced
- 1 large russet potato (or 2 medium-sized potatoes), cut into small cubes
- 1/2 cup roasted buckwheat kernels
- 3/4 cup dry red lentils
- 2 cups vegetable stock
- 1 tablespoon herbs de Provence
- 1/4 cup nutritional yeast
- 1/2 cup frozen corn
- 1/2 cup frozen peas
- salt and pepper
- breadcrumbs (optional)

1. Preheat the oven to 400°F (200°C).
2. In a pan or in an oven-and-stovetop-safe pot like a cast iron Dutch oven, sauté onion, carrot, and celery

   in butter or oil for about seven minutes; add garlic
   and potatoes. Add salt and pepper to taste.

3. After a few more minutes, add the lentils, buckwheat
   groats, herbes de Provence, and vegetable stock. Turn
   up the heat and bring just to a boil, stirring frequently.

4. Turn down and let simmer for 30 to 40 minutes,
   until the liquid has been absorbed and the lentils and
   buckwheat are cooked.

5. Add nutritional yeast, frozen corn, and frozen peas.
   Stir to combine. Taste; add more salt and pepper and
   more nutritional yeast, if desired.

6. If you've been using a sauté pan, transfer contents
   into a loaf dish and place into oven. If you've been
   using an oven-and-stovetop-safe vessel, bung it
   directly into the oven. You can top the dish with
   breadcrumbs before placing it in the oven, if you like.

7. Cook for 30 minutes at 400°F (200°C).

POMMES DAUPHINE

Adapted from a Kristina Razon recipe for *Serious Eats*.

Unlike other recipes in this book, this one takes a while to come together. About an hour and forty minutes—or up to two hours if you're pulling various elements of dinner together simultaneously.

The beauty of this *Serious Eats*–adapted recipe is that it calls for a low-starch potato variety and then takes specific steps to further reduce starch and moisture. This results in an incredibly light and crispy final product. A higher-starch potato will lead to a denser (and still delicious) result.

Serve with gravy and whatever you like eating with gravy. The pommes dauphine are a bit of a production, so it's nice to keep the other elements of the plate simple. (I started the gravy, for example, before starting the pommes dauphine—that way, it could hang out on low on another part of the stovetop while I focused on the pommes.)

- large Dutch oven or deep fryer
- thermometer suitable for deep-frying
- stand mixer with paddle attachment (optional but nice)
- medium-sized heavy-bottom pot
- wooden spoon
- spatula
- large bowl
- peeler
- knife
- slotted spoon, strainer, or spider

INGREDIENTS

For the choux pastry

- ½ cup milk
- 3 tablespoons (42 grams/1.5 ounces) unsalted butter
- pinch of salt
- ¼ cup plus 2 tablespoons gluten-free flour mix
  (or 64 grams/2.3 ounces all-purpose wheat flour)
- 2 large eggs at room temperature

For the potatoes

- 454 grams (two or three) russet potatoes, peeled and
  cut into cubes
- 1 teaspoon table salt
- 2 tablespoons (28 grams) unsalted butter, melted
- black pepper

For frying

- about 2 litres (67 fluid ounces) vegetable or canola oil

To make the choux pastry

1. In a medium-sized heavy-bottom pot, combine milk, butter, and salt.
2. Over high heat, stir until the mix comes to a boil.
3. Remove from the stove, and using a wooden spoon, tip in the flour and mix vigorously until smooth.
4. Return the pot to the stove, turning the heat down to medium-high, and continue to stir with the wooden spoon until the mix fully coheres and a skin forms on the bottom of the pot.
5. Transfer the dough to a stand mixer fitted with the paddle attachment, and beat for a few minutes until the mixture has cooled down a bit. It will still be warm.
6. Turn the mixer down to low, and add one egg. Once the egg is in the mixer bowl, turn the speed back up to medium. Once it's fully incorporated, add the second egg. Mix until the batter is transformed—it will be shiny and smooth.
7. Scrape down the sides of the mixer bowl with a spatula, and then use that spatula to give it a final small mix to incorporate the batter from the sides of the bowl.
8. Remove the paddle attachment from the mixer, and press plastic wrap directly against the surface of the dough to prevent a skin from forming while you move on to working on the potatoes.

To make the pommes dauphine

1. Give your medium-sized heavy-bottom pot a quick wash out.
2. Preheat your oven to 200°F (93°C). Place a wire cooling rack inside a baking sheet, and line it with a couple layers of paper towel.
3. Add your cubed potatoes to a large bowl; head to the sink and add cool water to the bowl. Swish the potatoes around, empty the water out, and repeat (probably three times) until the water runs clear.
4. Put the potatoes in the heavy-bottomed pot, cover with water, and add the salt. Bring to a boil, turn down a bit, and cook till fork tender (but not falling apart).
5. Drain in a colander, and rinse with hot water (to remove even more starch).
6. Add back to the pot and cook on low for a minute, tossing the potatoes around while you do so. This step dries them out.
7. Rinse and dry the large bowl you used to rinse the potatoes.
8. Rice the potatoes back into the large bowl. (You can also mash them with a fork, but ricing helps keep them light and fluffy.) Fold in the melted butter and the pepper with a stiff spatula.
9. Add the choux pastry into the bowl and fold it together with the potatoes. Reuse your plastic wrap to cover the mixture.
10. Add the vegetable or canola oil to the Dutch oven or deep fryer, and bring it to 340°F (170°C) over medium-high heat. This can be fiddly: I find I need to turn the burner down a bit as the oil approaches temp.

11. When you've hit 340°, grab a couple spoons. The dough is wet and sticky, and it's necessary to work quickly to get the batch into the oil at about the same time, so we're not looking for perfection. Plunge one spoon into the dough and swivel your hand in a little 360° turn, grabbing about a tablespoon of dough. Use the other spoon to scoop that dough from the first spoon and into the oil. Repeat until you have ten balls of dough in the oil. Cook them for three and a half minutes until they're golden brown.

12. When they're cooked, transfer them to the paper-towel-covered wire rack in the oven. Using a slotted spoon or strainer/spider, collect a few balls, allow the oil to drip back into the Dutch oven for a moment, and then open the oven and pull the rack out to transfer the dough. When I'm making pancakes and keeping them warm in the oven, I tend not to pull the rack out at all; in this case, your prepared wire rack and baking tray situation will cover the oven door, meaning any oil splatters will land on the paper towel and tray rather than on the oven door.

13. Repeat the process two or three more times until you've used up the dough.

the spectacle of the big bite

In 2011, for the *New York Times*, Jeff Gordinier wrote about the phenomenon of celebrity profiles that include a spectacle of voracious eating. The profiles, he wrote, generally feature a starlet of "slim and gamine proportions" thwarting reader expectations by ordering and eating a meal fit for a "hungry dockworker." He namechecks Jennifer Lawrence, Zoe Saldaña, and Cate Blanchett as profilees and calls out *Esquire*—a magazine he'd later work at for five years as the food and drinks editor—as a particularly frequent contributor to the genre. The phenomenon, Gordinier adds, is now so frequent it has a name: the "documented instance of public eating."

Unlike profiles focusing on actors losing or gaining weight for particular roles, the documented instance of public eating signals that a celebrity's thinness and beauty is something close to effortless. The idea of a thin woman eating voraciously in public is more palatable to many readers than a fat woman eating in public, or David Beckham's admission that Victoria Beckham has eaten the same low-calorie dinner of grilled fish and steamed vegetables for the past twenty-five years.

These profiles are a reflection of our culture's obsession with thinness and "obesity," our fixation on the idea that the morality of a person is clearly and bodily legible, an accumulation of "right" or "wrong" choices. What makes the documented instance of public eating so compelling that it became a trope is that it flouts this expectation, showing a "right" body making a "wrong" choice. The cool girl who stays thin while devouring burgers; the object of appetite showing that she has an appetite of her own. (The one thing I've never been sure about is whether we're supposed to acknowledge the effort made behind the scenes in order to enact this brief public show.)

But what is obviously gratuitous for a celebrity profile changes in meaning when the documented instance of public eating is a *chef*'s documented instance of public eating.

When we watch TV shows—or TikToks or Instagram reels—about cooking, the food is the point. Watching someone cook, we learn about ingredients and technique. We're also imagining what the finished product might taste like, what its textures might be.

Given that time and distance separate us from the food itself, we live vicariously through the chef's response. But the experience is different when it's Guy Fieri and a taco versus a thin attractive woman chef and whatever she has created.

And there are often dynamics at work similar to what Gordinier described—publicly visible appetite means something different depending on your gender, your size, your queerness, your race. It's never just about the food.

On *Two Fat Ladies*, Clarissa Dickson Wright and Jennifer Paterson putter to the seaside on a motorbike with a sidecar, cooking mussels on a portable stove in butter, wine, shallots, and parsley. They're miked as they crack open the shells and eat the plump little shellfish, their mouths smacking in pleasure.

Pouring honey into a pan, Nigella Lawson catches a drip from the jar with her finger, which she then puts to her mouth.

Guy Fieri is an easy pick for the unfussy version of the genre: watch five minutes of the Food Network and you'll see him turn the brim of his cap to the back to better sink his teeth into a burrito. Ditto the host of *You Gotta Eat Here!*, John Catucci, whose job parallels Fieri's—to wrap his mouth around stunningly large burgers, or pieces of fried chicken, embodying a zealous desire to taste.

Anthony Bourdain ate and drank heartily, usually while in conversation; in promotional photos for his shows, he's often caught as he's about to bring a pair of chopsticks or a spoon to his lips, making it seem like he is perpetually about to start a meal.

When Alex Guarnaschelli judges food on *Chopped*, she pokes, bites, evaluates. Her face shifts in a moment of pleasure from eating or, conversely, a moment of uneasy analysis. There are fewer women judges on *Chopped* than male judges; Guarnaschelli doesn't soften her feedback, isn't always kind, often wears shirts with sleeves. (Wearing sleeves is one indicator a woman is allowed to embody appetite without also being the object of it herself.)

On *$40 a Day*, Rachael Ray makes a little "mmm" sound, looking up at the ceiling. On *30-Minute Meals* and on her eponymous (and incredibly popular) TV show, she tended to say "Yum-o!" almost as frequently as "EVOO," being parodied for both. (Her on-camera exuberance for food is rivalled only by Guy Fieri's—but while Fieri has convincing defenders for his long-lambasted corniness, Ray doesn't. Instead, the comments on her older shows posted to YouTube zero in on the fact that her body is larger now than it was when she first started hosting food TV in her twenties.)

Padma Lakshmi shares an enthusiastic "mmm" as the spoon she's holding returns to her bowl. She eats a rib carefully, in a way that won't leave sauce on her face or much on her fingers—the way my nana would have taught me to eat a rib, if I hadn't been a stubborn vegetarian for most of the time I knew her.

Comparing Lakshmi and Lawson to schlumpy male chefs, you can come away thinking that both women are required to check more boxes and yet receive fewer opportunities in return. It's clear they also both enjoy the food they're tasting. But for Lawson—and for Lakshmi before she began her show *Taste the Nation*—there's a subtle, electric difference in the way the camera captures their enjoyment. Yes, we're meant to be imagining tasting what they are tasting. But the pleasure melts outwards, pausing on their bodies and sensuality. In a vacuum, that's fine. Viewed through a broader lens, why doesn't the camera make the same pauses for male chefs? Why is sensuality only allowable for women chefs who fit certain fairly narrow beauty parameters? And is it *required* of women chefs in a way that it is not required of male chefs? And where do non-binary, trans, and queer chefs fit into this paradigm, which feels so classically for the heterosexual male gaze? Finally, is this framing of attractive women chefs part of what limits, in the imaginations of studio executives, their career ambitions?

A long-time host of Bravo's *Top Chef*, successful cookbook author, and household name, Lakshmi had to pitch *Taste the Nation* several times before it was picked up by Hulu, flying to L.A. to do so on her own dime. She was pitching a *Diners, Drive-Ins and Dives* type show where she'd travel around the U.S. to explore immigrant contributions to American culture through food. "My show has been nominated for an Emmy every single year that I've been doing it," she told the *New York Times*. "All these networks that claim they want diversity—and here was *Taste the Nation*, a show about the diversity of our country, and they said no."

It's possible the exec Lakshmi referred to in that interview said no because they believed that it's easier to send a white man around the country to speak with the white bros we might misguidedly picture staffing all kitchens;[1] it's possible execs said no because they believed viewers, regardless of their own identities, can better see themselves tasting from the perspective of a white man than white men can see themselves tasting from the perspective of anyone else.

Ultimately, though, the result is the same: the closer one is to maleness and whiteness, the more one gets to be the avatar for exploration and tasting—with less of an expectation to be charming, perfectly coiffed, well-dressed, gorgeous.

But it wasn't always like this, and I'm unconvinced it's what viewers are really drawn to. The enduring personalities associated with TV cooking aren't necessarily classically attractive. There's space for them to be a bit odd, tall, fat, crooked-toothed, eccentric. It was a mistake to try to make cooking show hosts as blandly attractive and next-door relatable as the carpenters who built furniture for *Trading Spaces*.

In the moments when chefs perform the theatre of eating on camera—something Stanley Tucci describes in an essay about Julia Child as an act that "humanizes" famous people, makes us feel closer to them—I'm also thinking about the function of

---

1   Plenty of people of colour, and plenty of white women and non-binary people, work in the restaurant industry; what's true is that racism, sexism, and other barriers have led to underrepresentation of these groups in areas of the industry that carry more prestige—and pay more money. The majority of higher-level restaurant positions are occupied by white workers and a disproportionate percentage of these positions are held by white men. See Restaurant Opportunities Centers United, *Ending Jim Crow in America's Restaurants: Racial and Gender Occupational Segregation in the Restaurant Industry*, 2015, https://laborcenter.berkeley.edu/pdf/2015/racial-gender -occupational-segregation.pdf.

pleasure. Do non-male chefs get to publicly experience an exuberant, receptive kind of pleasure? Do women get to *keep* eating until they're satiated if they want to? Is a female chef's job just to make enjoyable food and then enjoy it? Or is her job, unlike Fieri's, in part to be consumable herself?

If a TV chef spits the food into a dump bucket at the end of a take, does it matter? If we want the hot white woman cook to stay youthful, impeccably thin, beautiful, can we also expect her eat voraciously? Is appetite only a desirable trait in a woman when it is presented as an impossible puzzle?

Of course, these questions are overly simplistic, and the enduring popularity of shows like *Two Fat Ladies* belie them. Dickson Wright and Paterson were popular when their series first aired and remain recognizable and well watched over two decades later. Rachael Ray, chef and author Joshna Maharaj points out when I speak with her, may be less popular with viewers than Guy Fieri because of a history of cultural appropriation in her dishes, which often take "shortcuts" to "simplify" them for white American audiences. Lakshmi's *Taste the Nation* was picked up for a second season, and Samin Nosrat is arguably the most beloved food writer and TV host working in North America today.

There is no universal viewer, no universal witness to appetite. There are only people making the food they themselves enjoy and sharing it with us. And then there is the filter—the way culture reflects what it imagines to be our desires.

When our viewing choices are more democratized through platforms like YouTube and TikTok and Instagram, the math changes. (Even though the algorithms still prioritize white creators.)

The ecosystem of creation on these platforms is more diverse than what you find on TV in a variety of ways: more women of colour, more trans cooks, more non-tokenizing and creative approaches to food. (Food Network's *Pioneer Woman*, going into its eleven billionth season and epitomizing the network's non-competition offerings, packs the punch and creativity of a dry piece of toast.) My personal favourites also tend to focus less on meat as the centre of each and every plate.

Some examples: on Instagram, as @BlackForager, Alexis Nikole forages, cooks, and eats whatever's edible in her surroundings: lilac cordial brewed using the wild yeast on the lilac flowers; veggie-bacon-wrapped hosta shoots; grape hyacinth extract that turns pink when added to lemonade. Her clips are generally about two minutes long and still manage to pack in followable recipes, foraging tips, and funny, sing-song asides.

Poppy O'Toole (@PoppyCooks), a Michelin-trained chef who lost her kitchen job during COVID, cooks potatoes obsessively, including variations on a fifteen-hour pressed and fried potato dish. Her cooking video style is one part food prep ASMR and one part voiceover, generally culminating in a crunch and an "ooh."

Richard Makin (@SchoolNightVegan) offers inventive vegan swaps for ingredients like anchovy paste, with a focus on technique; Bettina Makalintal (@crispyegg420) makes delicious bowls often featuring crispy eggs, tasty mushrooms, and crispy tofu; Afia Amoako (@EatWithAfia) cooks vegan versions of Ghanian foods like melon seed soup and jollof rice while sharing cultural, ecological, and historical information about ingredients like millet and sorghum; Ben Siman Tov (@BenGingi) bakes breads and says, "YASSS!"

Some of these cooks taste their food at the end of the video loop; some continue the video past the first taste, as if you're sharing the table with them; some enact a pre-eating ritual like breaking a cookie, or drawing a fork across an egg yolk until it flows like a small avalanche—more possible on TikTok or Instagram than TV because these platforms allow us to feel closer to the creator themselves, so these instances can become point-of-view stand-ins for *us* breaking, snapping, pulling, and poking.

Because the act of eating is necessarily simpler than the act of cooking, the tropes of eating and tasting in cooking videos become more evident. The theatre of tasting, done again and again, even on one's own channel, can begin to replicate the relatively narrow available options. How many times can a person crunch or "ooh"? Who's *not* going to try to take a more elegant or substantial or noteworthy bite knowing they're on camera, baring their dentistry to the world?

But it's also true that what you can find on Instagram often feels more genuine than most of what's available on food television—and that's true of the tasting as well as the cooking. Some cooks sidestep the whole process itself, opting, like Sohla El-Waylly often does, to let the viewer make the imaginative leap between seeing the food and dreaming of tasting it.

Do you usually watch your friends or family eat when you eat together? I don't. I'm usually focused politely elsewhere, making eye contact only when they've swallowed and are talking between bites. I've probably seen Nigella Lawson and Guy Fieri and Jamie Oliver eat on camera more than I've seen my partner, who I eat with three times a day, twenty-one times a week, in person.

By definition, it's a very normal thing to eat. But a less normal thing to perform the act of eating for others.

So the spectacle of the big bite will always be a spectacle, always a bit of theatre. It provides one lens through which to examine cultural expectations, trends, and the way food media has changed over time.

In its more democratic arenas, it has the power to unshackle desire and appetite from cultural conditioning—more people embodying what they want to embody, unreservedly, one big bite at a time.

trifling

Before I ever even thought of making Grandma Garcia's trifle recipe, I found myself buying a crystal dish from a thrift store in my small town. A few weeks later, I saw an even better trifle dish. It had a metal rim and little triangles and ridges like the back of a stegosaurus. I bought it and unceremoniously redonated the initial one I'd purchased, feeling only a mild twang of guilt.

Once I was in possession of the nicer trifle dish, it seemed only right to ask my Grandma Garcia for her recipe, like the dish was willing the dessert into existence. I knew the trifle took my GG several days to make, and I knew she used booze to make it—both the trifle and the rum cake she and my Granddad Ralph make at the holidays are boozy. I've eaten them both since I was a child, but this was the first time I felt called to recreate them.

Before my mid-twenties, I'm not even sure I would have told someone, if they'd asked out of the blue, that I *liked* trifle. It's composed of a base—sponge cake and jam—I can take or leave; a layer of tinned fruit, usually mandarin oranges, which I like okay; a layer of Jell-O, which I don't otherwise eat; a layer of vanilla custard, which I'd only otherwise eat if hospitalized;

and some finishing layers of whipped cream and fresh fruit (no gripes about either of those).

But the year before Sinclair was born, when Will and I were living in a tiny three-and-a-half in Little Italy in Montreal, and my paternal family were going to visit from Ontario for Thanksgiving, and my GG asked me what I'd like her to bring, I learned I missed her trifle the exact second I blurted it out, thoughtlessly: "Trifle, please." I tried to backtrack as soon as I said it. Not because I didn't want trifle, but because I realized how selfish it was. I can't eat gluten! It's a days-long preparation! How would she even transport it so far in the car?

My GG, then in her late seventies, figured it out. When we ate it, it reminded me of all the holidays we'd spent at her and Ralph's house playing cutthroat card games around their long dining room table.

It was only after I'd had a kid, moved back across the country, bought a house, and then bought two trifle dishes in succession that I finally asked GG for the recipe. She mailed it inside a card, on cardstock of its own. It read:

CUNLIFFE FAMILY TRIFLE
(OVER 100 YEARS OLD)

Simplified version

Day 1: Place pound cake, Swiss roll, or any sponge cake in bottom of large dish. (Can be stale.) Sprinkle generously with sherry or brandy.

Day 2: Open can of fruit—peaches, mandarin oranges, etc.—and place on cake base. Make a jelly, any flavour, using the juice to replace the cup of cold water called for in recipe. Stir well, and pour over the cake and fruit, cover and return to fridge to set.

Day 3: Carefully pour a can of custard over the above and smooth. Cover and return to fridge.

Day 4: Whip up, with electric beaters, a small carton of whipping cream and place on top of trifle. Decorate as desired—walnuts, maraschino cherries, etc.

I had no clue the recipe was so old. My GG later told me it had been handed down through the generations. My dad, who is good at holding onto family history even if he's terrible at baking, went into more detail: it came from my great-great-grandmother Esther Clough's mother, Sofia. "Esther was born in the 1880s as one of the children of Sofia's second marriage to William Clough," he texted me. "My gut says she got it likely from her mum, Harriet Mills Bradbury, but it was Sofia who first wrote it down."

Trifle itself has its roots in medieval custards and sixteenth-century fruit fools, which are made by incorporating stewed fruit into custard. By the eighteenth century, it looked more like it does today. By then, as our recipe suggests, it incorporated jelly and offered a way to use up stale biscuits. Initially, it used syllabub—milk or cream curdled with cider. Whipped heavy cream came later, via the Scots.

I'm currently in the process of changing my middle name, from my great-grandmother's first name to her maiden name, Cunliffe. I'm making the change for gender reasons, but I chose another of her names, one I felt more comfortable carrying on instead; the trifle is another smaller link I know I can carry on too. One I wasn't expecting.

Because I can't eat gluten and because I like making custard, my version unsimplified (or recomplicated) the trifle. Back to which generation in the past, I can't be sure. Custard powder has existed in the U.K. since the 1830s, and it would make sense if my great- and great-great- and great-great-great-grandparents cut whichever corners they could. They would have had a bunch of other things to prepare in the days leading up to trifle holidays. Long story short: I retained the store-bought Jell-O package but decided to make the jelly roll base and the custard myself.

DAY ONE

I found a gluten-free recipe for a sponge containing four U.K. large eggs, 110 grams of gluten-free flour mix, 110 grams of sugar, and 20 millilitres of milk. U.K. large eggs are equivalent to extra-large eggs in North America, and I only had large eggs. So I looked up the weight of a large U.K. egg minus its shell, multiplied by four, cracked five large Canadian eggs, whisked them together, and poured them into a bowl on a scale, holding back half an egg, or maybe a third of an egg, which went into a tiny little Tupperware and then into the fridge.

Jelly rolls look deceptively simple—a swirl of egg-leavened sponge encasing some raspberry or strawberry jam—but they're pretty hit or miss, especially if they're gluten-free. This recipe called for whipping the eggs with the sugar until it left a trail after detaching the whisk and drizzling the mixture over itself. It then called to have the flour sifted over top, and the milk added afterwards, being careful not to deflate the eggs and sugar. After everything was gently combined, it went into a sheet pan lined with parchment paper.

The roll baked quickly, taking around thirteen minutes. Jelly rolls need to be removed from the oven the second they spring back from a finger—and it really is easiest to tell with your finger, because your finger will communicate far more accurate data to your brain than an implement, but yes, if you're following along, this *does* mean putting your hand into the oven and onto a steaming hot sheet pan of cake. If the cake is done, and it's vanilla, it will have just a hint of goldenness around the edges. But you shouldn't trust goldenness as the measure of doneness: if the cake is truly and uniformly golden, it will probably crack when you roll it.

The rolling part is where things get truly tricky. Some recipes suggest sprinkling sugar onto an outstretched piece of parchment and quickly flipping the cake upside down onto it. In my experience, this results in a mangled cake. My preferred method is to have an outstretched sheet of parchment ready alongside my sugar container and a trivet. Working quickly, I took the sheet pan out of the oven, placed it on the trivet, sprinkled the *cake* with sugar, placed the new parchment paper on top, shielded my hands with tea towels, and flipped the pan over with the parchment covering it so that the parchment ended up on the counter with the cake and pan on top. Still working quickly, I removed the pan and placed it aside, chose a short edge, and rolled the cake up like a wayward little towel from the laundry.

The next step is to let the rolled-up sponge cake fully cool down on a wire rack, making sure, if you, too, have a cat who really loves eggy cake, to keep the cat away from the cake. Rolling the cake up while it's hot allows the cake to remember how to roll back up when it's cool, so you can spread it with jam or whipped cream or whatever you'd like to fill it with.

If you escape the making of this cake without any burns whatsoever, you're either highly skilled, or you've done it wrong.

On day one of my first attempt at making Grandma Garcia's trifle, I was pleased with my efforts. When it was cool, my sponge unrolled well, spread easily with jam, and rolled back up nice and smooth, with no cracks.

Later, after I'd lined the trifle dish with jelly roll slices, I dabbed on sherry with a pastry brush. There were a few slices left over, so I served them for dessert. And that is when I discovered that I had followed the recipe's insistence to not overmix the sponge cake batter a little too zealously. The jelly roll, while visually appealing, was studded with funny little bits of flour that had not been fully hydrated by the whipped egg and sugar mix. Disappointing! But not disappointing enough to turf the entire thing and start over.

DAY TWO

On day two, I poured a tin of mandarin oranges over a fine-mesh sieve, reserved the juice, topped the sponges with the oranges, whisked boiling water into a raspberry Jell-O packet, and added the mandarin orange juice. I cooled the Jell-O in the fridge for an hour, then poured it over a spoon for gentler distribution onto the orange slices and sponge. The cooling step and the spoon step are not included in the recipe, but both helped to ensure I didn't mangle or, worse, cause the complete disintegration of the sponge cake by power-washing it with hot liquid.

DAY THREE

On day three, I made the custard first thing after breakfast, following a recipe from the *Spruce Eats* called "Classic English Custard Sauce." It's specifically billed as being for trifle; it calls for milk and cream to be heated in a saucepan with a teaspoon of sugar and then used to temper six egg yolks that have been beaten with a third of a cup less one teaspoon of sugar. The mixture is added back to the saucepan with vanilla bean seeds and warmed gently on the stovetop until it coats the back of a spoon (meaning that if you dip the spoon into the custard and run your finger through the custard mix on the spoon, the line you draw will keep its boundaries).

This should not have been terribly difficult for me. I regularly make successful custard for churning into ice cream; I make pastry creams, which are similar but thickened with cornstarch; one of my favourite simple desserts is chocolate mousse, which is made by folding whipped cream into homemade chocolate custard. I followed the *Spruce Eats* recipe to a T. Even though I was certain I knew what it meant to warm the custard gently on the stovetop until it coated the back of the spoon, I used my thermometer just in case, bringing it to just over 170 degrees Fahrenheit. I strained it into a bowl, covered it with clingwrap, and asked my partner to put it in the fridge after it came to room temperature—I was running out to do errands. When I came home, I poured it onto the jelly layer.

Six hours later, it was not set at all. So I poured the custard back off the cake and Jell-O, into a stainless steel bowl, whisking in one tablespoon, and then two—the second may have been a mistake?—of cornstarch. I heated it over a pot of steaming water until it reached 175 degrees Fahrenheit. Bringing it back to room temp, I cooled it in the fridge.

Friends came over for dinner, thankfully not for trifle, and when they left, I tasted the custard, realized it was a bit grainy, decided the culprit was the cornstarch, and heated it for the third time, this time directly in a saucepan again. I decided if the egg scrambled, that would be fine: it would be the universe telling me this custard was cursed and I needed to start over. It didn't scramble. I let it thicken on the stovetop like pudding or, really, like pastry cream. It had seriously reduced in volume by this point. It was not perfect, but each scoop of the finished trifle would have so little custard-pudding-pastry-cream that I figured no one would notice that it was at best a five out of ten.

It was also on day three that I wondered why I was making this thing. Sure, vanilla custard is just one component of it, and Jell-O is also just one component, but I happen to dislike them both. There is an alchemy to all the layers coming together, I think. But I was also making it because I wanted to feel closer to my GG. I was conscious of the fact that she'd turned eighty-five last year, and that she would not remain hale and hearty and anxious and grumpy and funny forever. I wanted to get good at making her trifle while she was still around, so that when I was next in Ontario, I could make it for her.

I also wondered why I'd followed a North American recipe for custard on a website I find a bit uneven. In part, it's because of the egg size issue I had with the jelly roll. I wanted six large egg yolks to be equivalent, without any math or partial yolks, to the six large egg yolks I had. (Laziness! Chastened for my impertinence!)

After I spooned my thick custard-pudding-pastry-cream over my jelly layer and set the whole thing back in the fridge again, I immediately began looking up Mary Berry trifle recipes. Surely she had a recipe for a custard that would actually work in a trifle. A representative one of her trifle custards (she's made many over the years) calls for:

- 50 grams (2 oz) caster sugar
- 3 tablespoons cornflour
- 4 egg yolks
- 1 tablespoon vanilla extract
- 450 ml (15 fl oz) full-fat milk
- 150 ml (5 fl oz) double cream

On YouTube, I watch a 1975 clip of Mary Berry making a trifle for the TV show *Good Afternoon!* Host Judith Chalmers asks Mary Berry, as she is adding five tablespoons of sherry to pear juice and maraschino cherry juice to soak her sandwiched sponges, what she thinks of sherry substitutes. "I don't think it's a good idea to use them at all," Berry says, forecasting her later fondness for boozy desserts on *Great British Bake Off*.

In this clip, Mary heats half a pint of milk on the stovetop. "This is a vanilla pod, Judith," she says. "That's the real McCoy." She adds three egg yolks to a glass bowl, whisking in an ounce of sugar and a teaspoon of cornstarch. When the milk is hot, she tempers the egg mixture and places it back on the stovetop, where she cautions to cook it slowly. "It is quite tricky," she says. "You mustn't let it boil or become too hot. It must be very, very hot, so you can hardly put your hand in, and it must coat the back of a spoon. Then let it get cold, and then pour it on top, and it sets like that." Gently shaking her trifle bowl, Mary Berry demonstrates that her custard is firm, with just the hint of a wobble. I take notes.

DAY FOUR

On the fourth day, I whipped some cream, plopped it onto the top of the custard, and decorated the top of the trifle with raspberries. This is not canon according to my GG's recipe, but it is something I'm sure I've witnessed her do. I texted friends of ours, Jen and Peter, who live just up the hill from us: "Are you interested in . . . some trifle?" When Jen said yes, I added the caveat that neither the jelly roll nor the custard was perfect. "Oh, we've been following on Instagram," she wrote back. (I had been Instagramming, via the Stories function, my trifle journey.)

Later, after they visited, Jen texted again: "Tastes pretty freaking good to me!" If I were a more normal person, I think I would have found this satisfying. But I knew I'd be remaking the entire thing again the following weekend, because I needed to perfect the sponge and custard based on what I'd learned from my first attempt.

To prepare, I watched more people make trifles. On the TV show *This Morning*, I watched Phil Vickery make a retro trifle, for Christmas, to what were apparently the Queen's specifications: sponge sandwiched with jam, a ton of sherry, tinned mandarin oranges, Bird's Instant Custard, no Jell-O, decorative elements that would be at home at a 1970s dinner party. The hosts are Holly Willoughby and Phillip Schofield; Willoughby, I recognize from another clip, a clip where she tells chef Gino D'Acampo that if his pasta dish had ham in it, it would be "closer to a British carbonara," and in response, he tells her that if his grandmother had wheels, she would have been a bike. We're an anti-monarchist family, so it's a touch disappointing to discover so many similarities between our trifle and the Queen's, but very little has ever turned me off eating dessert. On *Ireland AM*, I watch Karl Clarke make a traditional sherry trifle, again for Christmas. His incorporates sherry into the Jell-O as well as dousing the sponge with it. For kicks, I watch Nigella Lawson make an Anglo-Italian trifle, not for Christmas, with a base of sponge and jam, amaretti biscuits, lemon liqueur, and a layer of glossy, jammy blackberries topped with a whipped mascarpone.

TAKE TWO

The following Friday, I tried again. I remade the same sponge but mixed it more thoroughly. After watching dozens of clips of people in Ireland and England make trifle, I'd learned of something called "trifle sponge," which appeared to be the same sheet pan sponge I'd been baking but cut into small rectangles, bisected through the centre of the crumb, and sandwiched back together with jam, instead of being made into a jelly roll. It was a good thing I decided to do this before I made the second sponge, because even though I baked it for the exact same number of minutes as last time, it came out a hair too golden to roll.

When it was cool, I used a bread knife to gently turn the sponge into two layers and then a cheese knife to spread the raspberry jam. It was a rare Friday when my partner was working an evening shift; I tried to take my child out for sushi but the wait times were too long, and so I plied her with sponge scraps. "Did you make the jam yourself?" she asked, chewing. No, no, I did not.

When I shared the process pics from my first attempt with Grandma Garcia, she doled out compliments but also said the sherry should be drizzled! generously! and not dabbed. Which made sense, because the first trifle did not taste of sherry as much as it should have. So after I'd created two layers of little rectangles of trifle sponge at the bottom of the trifle dish, I poured some sherry into a pottery creamer and drizzled generously.

The next day, after swimming lessons, Sinclair and I went to the grocery store to get more mandarin oranges, whipping cream, and eggs. The rec centre is closest to the grocery store that carries organic dairy in glass bottles, which I've developed a taste for; the double nice thing about this cream is that it's 36 percent, even higher than the 33 percent available in cartons. (And it's a true 500 millilitres, unlike the carton, which comes in at 473.)

On day two, I again poured the tin of mandarin oranges over the sieve, reserved the juice, topped the sponges with the oranges, whisked boiling water into raspberry Jell-O, and added the mandarin orange juice. I cooled the Jell-O in the fridge for an hour, then poured it over a spoon and onto the orange slices and sponge. I felt like this was a step I could do sleepwalking— but then it's this type of hubris that leads to mistakes.

The morning of day three, I took what I'd learned from Mary Berry and made the custard recipe for her "celebration trifle." It came together easily and reached the perfect consistency. I strained it, pressed plastic wrap lightly onto the top to prevent it from developing a film, let it come to room temperature on the counter, and then cooled it in the fridge for a couple hours before pouring it on top of the Jell-O layer.

At dinner, I whipped some of the 36 percent cream with sugar, added some vanilla extract, dolloped it on top of the custard, and smoothed it out. Then I added blackberries.

It was perfect. The sponge stood up well, and this time around, I had been generous enough with the sherry. The proportions were correct; the custard was delicious. The blackberries were nice and tart, and nothing was too sweet.

It tasted exactly like what I'd expect from Grandma Garcia's trifle, and I felt like I'd learned a new magic trick. The only step remaining is to take everything I've learned a few thousand kilometres east, so I can make it for her. Only then will I really learn how she feels about my version and the idea that I'll be carrying it on.

the failure of the peppers

On a warm summer day, I bike to Blueberry Commons, where I've been volunteering every Friday. At the end of the nine-kilometre ride, which features a forest trail and a somewhat punishing hill, I turn onto King Avenue. On this street, there are a number of professionally printed signs declaring their opposition to an application to rezone the Blueberry Commons lots to allow for a cohousing project—and a few more signs, planted in the lawns of the wilder-looking houses, in support. The Blueberry Commons farm is on one of its conjoined lots; its new cohousing units are set to be built on a second lot that has stood fallow as a meadow for years. The street features a mix of small-scale agriculture and residential housing, like much of the Wildwood neighbourhood, located on the territory of the Tla'amin Nation in what is currently known as Powell River, B.C. Most of the lots are large—maybe a half acre or an acre—and some, like Blueberry Commons, are even larger.

This is the case for the farm's closest neighbours, too; they have a horse paddock. When I look over to check out the horses, like I do most Fridays, I see a juvenile black bear in the paddock with them. The curious bear, rebuffed by a horse, turns its attention towards me. And in a blink, the bear is running in my direction. My first instinct—to pedal faster—is the wrong instinct. My second instinct is to dismount, stand behind the bike, clap my hands, and tell the bear it has to stop and turn around. The bear, looking dejected—it just wanted to investigate, maybe play—turns around and lopes off. When it's safely gone, I get back on my bike and ride, this time pretty slowly, towards the farm, turning down its bumpy, rutted lane as my heart rate begins to return to normal.

On the lot at the east end of King Avenue, there is a little farm stand, with some parking. Up behind it, the fallow meadow. The lot at the north end features the old farmhouse, where Ron Berezan, a certified permaculture teacher who runs the farm, lives. The farm lane leads north past an herb garden and beehives on the left, the wash station and cold storage on the right, and, at the end of the lot, a meadow and three-quarters of an acre of U-pick blueberries on the left and a two-acre market garden on the right. The farm supports a CSA box program and supplies vegetables to the community through the farm store and a couple of locally owned grocery stores. It also draws people: cohousing members, volunteers like me, and kids from the local school, visiting with their teachers.

I did not start volunteering out of the goodness of my heart, or even a desire to contribute to community food security. I started volunteering halfway through the season, one week into July, after I threw a potted bell pepper plant out my greenhouse front door and onto the driveway, where it shattered.

The peppers, which were initially growing well, had developed soft spots—maybe blossom end rot from overwatering, maybe anthracnose, a fungus that thrives in warm, moist conditions. I'd been content with how the peppers were growing, and the season's early heat meant we were in line to get a large crop. The soft spots found me at a mental health nadir, and they felt like the last straw: my snap peas had powdery mildew; my container-planted tomatoes, even the cherry tomatoes, had blossom end rot; my eggplants had a spider mite infestation; and cabbage moths had deforested my purple sprouting broccoli seedlings—twice.

I took the soft spots personally. The peppers had failed because *I* was a failure. Someone who'd had beginner's luck the first couple seasons and would now need to contend with reality. A person who'd built the entirety of their self-worth on their accomplishments and was now accomplishing nothing other than a waste of soil and time. In that moment of overwhelming frustration, temporary self-hatred, a wave of anger I couldn't quell, I swore and lobbed the pepper plant.

In the aftermath—apologizing to my bewildered child and partner and cat, sweeping the soil up, rinsing and recycling the shards of plastic—I realized I couldn't continue the way things were. That same day, I joined an online peer support group for bipolar people, and I emailed Ron Berezan at Blueberry Commons. That week, I joined the bipolar support group. Two weeks later, I was volunteering on the farm. Both acts were in service of two questions: What would it take to get better? What would it take to not take it so personally when my crops failed?

"I am ready for spring but not the passage of time," I'd written in my garden diary earlier that year. And: "my desire for it to be March for gardening-related reasons is heavily compartmentalized from my desire for time to stop just Pac-Man chomping through all the days and months as I'm trying to live them during this godforsaken pandemic."

Initially, gardening had offered me a way to ground my natural tendencies towards anxiety and depression by allowing me to align myself with the rhythms of the seasons, of plants and insects and soil and rain and sun and weather. Growing plants from seed and supporting them as they grew and cooking with their fruits felt literally transformative.

In my third year, this was intermittently true and not true. Sometimes tending the garden felt like a gift; other times, it felt like another chore on a long list of daily, never-ending chores. A box to check or, worse, a task that further sapped my depleted energy and willpower.

When I texted my friend Nola about the failures of my garden, she told me to complain away. "It's very disheartening," she wrote back. "If it helps, know that every farmer at every scale has had that experience. Some years, you grow more knowledge. Some years, more food."

Nola shared a story: one year, a permaculture gardener wanted to visit her tea garden. The gardener knew Nola used to be a permaculture designer, so she felt it needed to be good—"but everything was just a pile of weeds and some of the plants were really struggling." Nola told her friend not to come. When the friend pressed her, she confessed about the state of her garden. "You'd be surprised what four hours of work side by side with a friend can accomplish," Nola's friend told her. "It made an incredible difference," Nola told me. "On the land and in my head."

Bill Mollison, who coined the term permaculture, defines it as "the conscious design and maintenance of agriculturally productive systems which have the diversity, stability, and resilience of natural ecosystems." His definition also folds in people and community: permaculture is "the harmonious integration of the landscape with people, providing their food, energy, shelter, and other material and non-material needs in a sustainable way." "Non-material" comes at the end of a rather long and practical list, but it's a significant inclusion: we only truly build resilient systems when those systems nourish us spiritually and bolster the connective tissues of our communities.

It's not really sustainable, or a reflection of a well-functioning ecosystem, to approach a garden so individualistically, as if it is a report card. I'd learned much of what I was practising from watching YouTube videos and consulting agricultural extension materials created by American universities. This education was invaluable, as was the connection I felt directly with the plants and insects and soil in my garden. But at a certain point, what had felt intimate began to feel isolating. I realized I needed to broaden my connections—to learn from others and bolster my participation in community, in person. I wanted to see what mitigation techniques other organic growers were using to ward off pests and diseases. I needed to see how other people were surviving and thriving and failing and picking themselves back up again.

Blueberry Commons' market garden is set up in long east-west rows over its two acres. Over the season, Ron tells me, the goal is to earn about a thousand dollars per row. On my first day volunteering, I pick buckets and buckets of snow peas, dumping them into rectangular blue harvest containers. As I leave, I see a woman in a beekeeping jacket tending to the bees. When I get home, I cut down and remove my pea plants, which have developed powdery mildew and are no longer producing. I leave their roots in the ground to add nitrogen to the soil. Using a machete, I hack the plants into pieces and toss them onto the compost pile.

The next week, I've just had my second COVID shot and am feeling lethargic, so I take the bus up to the farm. I pick Lacinato kale, dwarf curly kale, and chard. The fields are alive with white cabbage moths, the same moths that have been feasting on my broccoli sprouts in the greenhouse at home. One of the cohousing members picks me up as I'm walking home; I stuck to the highway instead of taking the forested switchback trail in order to avoid a bear and cub.

I meet a new friend, Lauren, pronounced like Sophia Lauren, an artist who likes to bike tour. She's been working on founding a lavender farm of her own but works at Blueberry Commons as well.

By late July, the farm's shelling peas and snow peas are still cropping but beginning to dwindle—more effort for fewer buckets. It's hot out. In the field, the peas and melons are abuzz with bees.

When I need to seek shade, a cohousing member teaches me how to braid softneck garlic to store in the rafters of the wash station and cold storage building. As we braid, she tells me about how a health scare when she and her husband were working abroad in their younger years led them to eventually purchase a sailboat and travel the world by sea. Now that they're older and settled again, cohousing is appealing for community and food production reasons.

In the field, Lauren and I chat as we prune tomato plants to encourage them to focus on growing flowers and fruit rather than foliage. After eating lunch in the shade, I go home and attend to my own tomato plants, which have begun to produce and to outgrow the six-foot-tall supports I've set up for them. The cherry tomatoes are ripe earlier than normal this year. The heat also leads to earlier crops for my lemongrass, basil, tomatoes, eggplants, poblanos, string beans—and the bell peppers, which have outgrown their soft spots.

Often, I find myself completing a task on the farm, biking home, and spending the afternoon on the same task at home— an echo at a quieter scale.

At the farm, I sort six full bins of cucumbers into small, for pickling whole; medium, for slicing and pickling; and large, for selling to eat raw. As I harvest my own cucumbers, we eat Greek salad, or tomatoes and cucumbers with mozzarella, basil, and balsamic vinaigrette. I make sweet quick pickles and cucumber kimchi. Sometimes, it feels a bit silly, this repetition. But I stick with it. I've oriented so much of my life towards making every moment of labour count towards a paycheque. It's embedded in my mindset, in the way I approach efficiency at work, in the way I internalize an employer's goals and standards. Some days it is difficult to make myself wake up and bike to the farm; some days, left to my own devices in the field, I feel as sad or devoid of feeling as I do at home. But volunteering begins to free me from the overarching obsession with productivity that exacerbates my mental illness. Volunteering, whatever I can offer is a bonus. If I lose thirty-eight seconds admiring the way a slug is resting in a head of broccoli the way a human would sit in the crook of a tree, I feel no guilt.

In August, I harvest summer squash at the farm—dark green zucchini, yellow zucchini, Romanesco, crookneck, and pattypan—after reinflating a wheelbarrow tire using my bike pump. I can hear lambs and turkeys beyond the western edge of the field.

The squash leaves scrape and prickle and cut my forearms and shins and calves. As I bike home, it rains, and the rain mixes with my sweat, and every bare inch of scratched skin sings out in pain. It should bother me more than it does; instead, the feeling of the rain on my face and the nettle-like stinging on my limbs is invigorating, like a free spa treatment. The raindrops, collecting, leave clean trails on my legs, which have been primed with a fine layer of mud and silt.

My summer and winter squash plants have begun to develop powdery mildew; the farm's have too. I study tips and tricks to mitigate it, removing the affected leaves and being careful to water the ground around the plant, rather than the leaves. But I also accept that it's a common late-season problem, not a personal failing.

Each Sunday afternoon, at the beginning of my bipolar support group, we rate our moods on a scale that accommodates both depression and mania. We share and offer each other feedback and support. At the end of the session, we rate our moods again. Occasionally, for me, the number doesn't budge. But usually, after listening and talking—sometimes more, sometimes less—I feel better.

Most days when I volunteer, if I rated my mood before I went into the field and then again afterwards, I'd find that it had improved. At first, I thought what gardening was teaching me was patience—to learn how to put in small daily effort for a reward that would come much later. I also thought it would help me slow down, appreciate the role of each passing season, stop catastrophizing about death and mortality, and come to respect the power of dormancy and re-emergence. And it has. But the lessons keep coming. A crop failure, for example, is a bit like a relapse. In learning how to accept these failures, I can also learn a bit about how to accept myself.

In September, I use a little sickle to harvest cabbages. It's serrated, with a red handle. The days are finally growing cooler and cloudy. Lauren asks me if I'd like to participate in a casual triathlon her friend is organizing. It will begin with a 1.5-kilometre swim in Lund, followed by a forty-kilometre bike ride back to Powell River, finishing with a ten-kilometre run. I say sure.

In October, a third-grade French immersion class visits for an hour to pick sugar pie and Jack Be Little pumpkins. The pumpkins are slick with mud, and the kids compete to see who can carry the heaviest ones. We place them into wheelbarrows and then line them up on tarps at the top of the field. The meadow just south of the blueberries has been turned into a pumpkin patch, which features a few large pumpkins the farm has been trying to guard from the neighbourhood bears. On the weekend, the pumpkins we harvested will be set up in this field, available for purchase.

Later, after the class has left and Lauren and I are picking the last hot peppers of the season, we hear gunshots. One of the nearby farms is harvesting its pigs. At the far end of the field, though Thanksgiving approaches, the turkeys are still strutting about unbothered, searching for worms and grubs in the grass.

By mid-October, Lauren has finished her season at the farm, and mine is winding up too. The triathlon, which I decided to swim and bike but not run, prompted us to meet every Sunday morning with some other new friends for a cold ocean dip.

At home, I harvest handfuls of bell peppers to augment the jalapenos from the farm and from my CSA box in a fermented hot sauce I'm making. I add slices of carrot and chunks of onion for flavour, placing everything in mason jars and adding carefully measured salt water, and a Ziploc bag full of water to weigh the vegetables down and keep them submerged.

It's only a few days later, checking on the ferment, that I realize this act of processing has closed a loop: these peppers began and ended a particular cycle of life in my garden, as well as marked the beginning and the soft end of the worst of my depression.

As I roll up to the farm on my own last day, it finally clicks for me that the space consists of two overlapping ecosystems— the food that's growing, and the social ecosystem of workers and volunteers. I'm a vanishingly small part of it, but I'm still a part of it. The smallness is a comfort: it's not all on me. Larger functioning systems compensate and rebalance and adjust. In this framework, the goal is not perfection or achievement. It's symbiosis and balance.

FERMENTED HOT SAUCE
Adapted from a recipe from *Feasting at Home*

I've mentioned elsewhere in this book that I have chronic gastritis. In addition to avoiding gluten, I drink very little alcohol and limit coffee and spicy foods. So I usually use poblano peppers or a mix of jalapeno peppers and bell peppers. It's a choose-your-own-spiciness type of hot sauce.

A note on salt: Sea salt, pickling salt and kosher salt are the best options for this recipe. Avoid iodized salt, which might inhibit fermentation. Also avoid anything too fancy—it's just not necessary.

A note on salt water: From everything I've read, the fermentation window occurs in a solution of salt water that contains between 2 percent and 5 percent salt. Anything below that and harmful bacteria will grow; anything above that will inhibit fermentation. This recipe gets you just above 2 percent. An alternative method for figuring out how much salt you need is to place your vegetables into your tared fermentation container, cover them with water, and then weigh the mixture. Multiply the weight of the vegetables and water by 0.025 to get the weight of the salt you'll need, and you'll end up with a brine just south of 2.5 percent salt.

INGREDIENTS

- 1,183 grams (42 ounces) water
- 25 grams (1 ounce) salt
- 454 grams (16 ounces) peppers
- 1 medium unpeeled carrot
- 6 cloves of garlic
- 1 small onion (or ½ large onion)

1. Stir the salt into hot water (hot from the tap is fine) until it's dissolved, and let the water come back to room temperature.
2. Cut the peppers into large chunks—around two by two inches, or a bit larger—and remove the seeds, pith, and ribs.
3. Slice the carrot and garlic into thin coins.
4. Quarter the onion lengthwise.
5. Mix up the vegetables and pack them into a fermentation crock or mason jars. Pour the saltwater brine over the veggies, making sure they're covered. I'll often retain a couple nice large pieces of pepper to place on top of the veggie mix—or you can use a big kale leaf, or cabbage leaf. This basically ensures that none of the smaller bits will float up above the brine and touch the air. You want everything to be immersed.

6. If you need more brine, mix more at a ratio of 100 grams of water to 2.5 grams of salt (4 ounces water to 0.1 ounces salt).

7. Weigh down the vegetable mix with clay fermentation weights, or if you are using mason jars and don't have weights, fill a Ziplock bag with water and place it on top of the veggie mix. Cover the crock with its lid, or if using mason jars, cover with cheesecloth or a tea towel and an elastic band.

8. Place the crock or mason jars in a cool, dry, dark place—the back of a cupboard or in a basement.

9. Check for fermentation on day five. The brine should be cloudy. If you shimmy the container back and forth, you should see bubbles come to the top of the brine. Fermentation happens more slowly if it's quite cool in your house. I usually leave mine to ferment for another couple days. But if you have a cloudy brine and see bubbles, you can choose to move to the next step at five days.

10. Next, set a colander over a large bowl—you want to save the brine. Strain the vegetables, and place them into a food processor or blender. Start by adding one cup of the brine, and add more later if you'd like a thinner sauce. Blend until you reach your desired consistency. I keep mine a bit chunky, like a mash; I do this by pulsing the mix in a food processor. But you can also blend until it's fully smooth.

11. Place in squeeze bottles with the tip open, or a jar with a loosened lid, and store in the fridge. Fermentation continues after the initial five to seven days; leaving the tip open or the lid loosened allows gases to escape. A sealed container may explode, in particular if it's left at room temperature.

give us this day
our daily beans

On Saturday mornings when I was a kid, my mother was usually at work, and my father was responsible for making sure we were clothed, fed, and washed. If you met my gregarious father, he might tell you he's great at making a stir-fry, or perhaps that he drinks a smoothie every day. I suspect he's stretching the truth; the last time I stayed at his apartment, I nosily discovered a film of dust on the blender and extra-nosily rooted through his pantry, finding a packet of gravy mix that expired two decades ago.

When he took my brother and me train-watching (exactly what it sounds like), he bought us McDonald's and let us run free in the botanical gardens close to the bridge where he most liked to see trains chug by so he could record their reporting numbers in a little book.

On days when there were Premier League soccer games featuring Manchester United, breakfast was usually beans on toast. Most often Heinz Original Beans in Tomato Sauce, without pork, on toast; sometimes the ones with pork, and sometimes the ones in molasses. A more frequent substitute was store-brand baked beans in tomato sauce, which were much cheaper. I remember them going for forty-nine cents a can at No Frills in the late '90s and early 2000s. (They're $1.19 as I write this in late January 2023.)

My dad likes his with Worcestershire sauce and other adulterations. I like mine the way they come in the can. My brother doesn't really like them at all, and often opted for cereal. My dad would heat up two cans in an oblong plastic Tupperware in the microwave, toasting six pieces of bread. One and a half cans and four slices for him; two slices and a half can for me. I disliked margarine, which was what we had at our house, so I had mine on plain toasted bread, letting the beans soak in until the bread had softened from the sauce. Today, my household contains salted butter; even better, the bean sauce mixes with the butter and becomes just a little richer.

In my younger, poorer, not cooking for my family years, I ate beans on toast with some carrot sticks on the side anywhere from once to four times a week. I still eat them today—on toast and incorporated into the very humble vegetarian shepherd's pie recipe I developed (recipe on page 125).

Full of fibre and protein, they are a cheap, easy meal; if I was asked, on a TV show like *Top Chef*, to make my "comfort food," baked beans are the food I would think of first before coming up with something I could actually serve to the judges. (Could I serve baked beans? I can make a convincing homemade dupe, but it takes hours longer than the twenty minutes cooks are usually allotted for these challenges.) I also might be the last person in my family who eats them regularly; Will and Sinclair don't like them, and my brother never did.

I've taken their existence for granted my whole life. It's only in considering their familial demise that I become curious about their history and the way they became a cultural touchstone for us.

The story of how baked beans became iconic in the U.K., like many iconic British things (tea! chutney!), begins elsewhere. Navy beans—a small white bean and a variety of *Phaseolus vulgaris*, which includes other common beans like pintos, green beans, black beans, and kidney beans, but not soybeans (*Glycine max*) or scarlet runners (*Phaseolus coccineus*)—are used to make them. *Phaseolus vulgaris* is native to what's currently known as the Americas and was first domesticated over five centuries ago; the bean had been developed into many different varieties and traditionally grown alongside corn and squash in many cultures, before colonizers stepped foot here. Europeans had favas and chickpeas and lentils pretty early, but it wasn't until the sixteenth century that they got the common bean.

Today, Brits eat more Heinz baked beans than anyone else on the planet. But the dish probably emerged from similar First Nations dishes, which were most likely made with maple syrup and sometimes venison and then adopted by hungry settlers, before being subsumed into industrialized production under Henry John Heinz and the H.J. Heinz Company, which began producing tinned baked beans in 1895 in Pittsburgh.

Heinz had made a trip to England about a decade earlier, cold-calling the head of the grocery department for Fortnum & Mason of London in 1886. The grocer began carrying Heinz items such as bottled horseradish sauce. Tinned baked beans made it to England in 1899, according to one source, and 1901, according to another, initially as a luxury import item. In 1928, the company began producing tinned beans in Harlesden, a district in northwest London; the price came down, and the product gained popularity.

It's unclear when, exactly, the New England–style beans exported from the U.S. changed recipes—but eventually the beans were adapted to suit British tastes, omitting molasses, maple syrup, and brown sugar for a tomato-based sauce.

From 1941 to 1948, tinned beans were rationed on the points system in the U.K. Coupon rationing covered staples like milk, eggs, butter, bacon, and ham. Points rationing was more flexible: each person received a certain number of points to use on a variety of essentials, beginning with canned meats, fish, and beans, and later extending to things like biscuits, grains, cheeses, dried eggs, and dried fruits. This is also when the beans lost their pork and became mostly vegetarian—why waste extra ration points?

Tinned beans ranged in value from three to eight points from the time point system rationing was introduced in 1941 (four points per pound) to 1944 (three points per pound) to 1947 (eight points per pound) to 1948 (six points per pound). The number of points citizens were allotted varied over the course of the rationing period—starting with sixteen in 1941, later rising to twenty-four, and then back down to twenty. (When I ask my Grandma Garcia if she remembers beans being rationed, she says no. She was only three in 1941, she reminds me.)

Today, Heinz Beanz—the U.K. version—are made in a factory in Wigan, in Greater Manchester, that claims the title of largest food processing plant in Europe. The navy beans used to make them are still imported from North America, and the tomatoes for the sauce are mostly grown in Spain and Portugal. The beans are checked for quality and then blanched for rehydration purposes, but the actual cooking process occurs after they're sealed into the can with the tomatoes and spices. The cans themselves are cooked in high-pressure steam.

Learning about the history of baked beans makes me wish I liked the ones with maple syrup or molasses or even pork. I could spin this off into an exploration of "authenticity" in food, but the truth is that authenticity is complicated and messy, and many foods and recipes are pluralized in a way that *is* authentic. It's important to understand relationships of power and colonialism, and the movement of different foods and food cultures through history. But ultimately, tinned beans in tomato sauce are the ones more familiar to me; they're my comfort food, even if they're a Frankenfood, a sloppy-looking hodgepodge of tan and brown that left this place for England only to come back again.

A further complication is that my Canadian taste buds aren't actually accustomed to Heinz Beanz. No, like many things with complicated colonial histories—spellings in English, for example—the Canadian beans I eat are a bit of a North American–British hybrid.

To explore this, I walk up to my local Save-On-Foods and buy two tins of Heinz beans in tomato sauce. The first comes from the British imports section: a turquoise tin reading "Heinz Beanz" on sale for $3.99 (or $3.49 if you have a Save-On card). On the other side of the aisle, for $2.49 (card price $1.89) are the Canadian beans in tomato sauce—my personal standard-bearer. Also in a turquoise tin, but reading "Heinz Beans Original."

At home, I open the tins (pop top for the U.K. beans, can opener for the Canadian) and arm myself with a fork. The U.K. version tastes more tomatoey. The beans are firmer, and there's more definition between the beans and the sauce. The Canadian beans are noticeably sweeter, less tomatoey, and just the faintest bit mushier—like the bean starch has leeched into the sauce a little more readily.

The U.K. ingredient list: beans (51 percent), tomatoes (34 percent), water, sugar, spirit vinegar, modified cornflour, salt, spice extracts, herb extract.

The Canadian: water, white beans, tomato purée, sugar, salt, calcium chloride, spice, mustard, onion powder, garlic powder.

In the U.K., the "spice mix" is apparently a closely guarded secret. In Canada—for allergy reasons?—we're willing to admit it contains mustard, onion, and garlic. I'm convinced I taste a hint of cloves, so I google and find cloves included, alongside Worcestershire sauce, in a number of dupe recipes.

My taste test confirms that I prefer the sweeter Canadian version. It also makes me reflect on the specific place these beans hold as a staple—mainly because after I have a few forkfuls, I need to decide on how we'll eat the remainder of the tins.

These days, we mostly eat dried beans. The pandemic solidified my movement towards dry goods and a full, stocked pantry, inspiring me to bulk-order twenty-five-kilo sacks of pintos and black beans. The pintos I cook fairly simply, incorporating sautéed garlic, onions, carrot, and green pepper and serving them over rice or polenta, with sour cream and salsa and homemade fermented hot sauce. The black beans, we use in anything from veggie burgers (the trick is to lay the cooked beans out on a baking sheet and dry them out a bit before incorporating them into the other ingredients for the burger) to soup to enchiladas. I use the Crock-Pot method, which sometimes calls, depending on the bean, for soaking and boiling for a short period before slowly cooking over the course of the day, the lid rocking gently on the porcelain when it reaches its highest heat, the house filling with the smell of stewed beans.

I cook favas, kidney beans, black-eyed peas, scarlet runners—anything going. And I love these beans. But I usually plan to make them the night before, setting up the dry ingredients in the Crock-Pot and sautéing any precooked elements when I make that night's dinner. They serve one function, and tinned baked beans serve another.

Because as a processed food, tinned beans are a cure-all for being both out of money *and* time. They are—still!—what I make when I'm hungry and tired and penny-pinching, in search of something that will take five minutes to prepare and still satisfy and satiate me. They are a cultural hangover from my dad's side of the family, both of our recent roots in England and a reminder of times when food insecurity was pressing for us, when we worked too much for too little money. But a reminder, too, of the calmer pockets of my childhood, of slow mornings with my dad, and the power of finding comfort where we can.

a taste for finery

Do you remember the first time you cut open a cantaloupe? I was sixteen and working at my best friend's father's produce store, which had a salad bar. My mother and her father were having an affair at the time, and while we worked at the store, they were usually drinking together at a nearby bar. My best friend's chipper Christian uncle worked at the store, as well as her grandmother Jean, who did not eat until dinner, subsisting on cigarettes and four-cream extra-large coffees from Tim Hortons. The store is closed now, and Jean is dead, so it's safe to tell you that she smoked in the kitchen.

From Jean, who was generous and kind but also deeply grumpy, I learned many of my first cooking lessons. I'd already worked prep at Tim Hortons, which at the time still made doughnuts in-house; I didn't make the doughnuts, but I peeled and chopped apples for the fritters, made strawberry tarts, and whipped cream cheese blocks in a giant industrial mixer to soften and aerate them before portioning them into individual cups for the sandwich station.

Mostly, Jean just told us what needed to be done to refill the salad bar. Her recipes lived in a binder and were detailed and clear, sometimes with additional notes in the margin, in a spidery hand (Jean's) or a very neat semi-cursive (chipper uncle's). But Jean sometimes dropped in a bit of additional information, like the beginning of a verbal crumb trail. It was from her, for example, that I learned to boil potatoes for potato salad skin-on. Their peels crack and come off easily afterwards—and you have to peel them while they're warm, in fact as hot as you can bear to handle, so that the outer layer of the potato blends effectively with the mayo in the dressing.

Jean was most likely there when I cut open my first-ever cantaloupe, and I would have hidden my surprise at discovering it was not in fact a solid mass of orange inside but had a large cavity that contained ribs of seeds. She would have shown me, rather than described in words, how to scoop out those seeds and slice the cantaloupes into moons and then chunks. Small enough to fit in one's mouth, but the less surface area, the better—they'd keep longer that way.

Before I brought the cantaloupe out to the salad bar, I ate a piece. Because the salad bar was in a produce store, the melons we used for it were usually properly ripe. The cantaloupe was fragrant and sweet, a bit floral. More complex than watermelon, which I'd eaten before, and a very different texture. At the Tim Hortons, we could eat Timbits for free, but that grew old fast. Snacking on Jean's salad bar offerings as I prepared them did not. Her potato salad was perfect, salty and tangy and simple with the crunch of celery and green onions. Her pasta salad used chicken stock in the otherwise straightforward dressing. Everyone (except me, I never tried them) loved her devilled eggs, and she had very clear instructions about how to cook them in order to avoid a green-grey ring around the outside of the yolk. (Making devilled eggs also marked the first time I ever used a pastry bag, which required a certain finesse and was incidentally the way you'd find out if you'd gotten the consistency of the filling right.)

But free access to cantaloupe was by far the best thing about working at the store. Each one tasted a bit different. Every single fruit offered a lesson about how to understand the signs of underripeness, ripeness, overripeness. An overripe cantaloupe tasted a bit like Sharpie. Not pleasant, but curious, and not entirely unpleasant. Unripe cantaloupes were firmer and tasted like little more than agave-sweetened fibre water. The best cantaloupes were the Ontario-grown ones we got in the summer, because they were picked closer to ripeness, and their flavour and texture were complex and tender, something like malted honey transmuted into melon.

I started working at the salad bar because I wanted to spend more time with my best friend—and because I don't have a personality suited for public-facing roles in entry-level jobs, such as retail. What kept me working in kitchens, though, was the food. We didn't make anything upscale for the salad bar, just the kinds of things you'd find at a blue-collar catered lunch for someone's retirement, or a stag and doe someone might hold in the community room of the local hockey arena. But by working there, I got to access new tastes, new textures, new experiences I wouldn't have otherwise. It made me want more.

For chef, activist, and author Joshna Maharaj, culinary school offered a different type of lesson—namely, that there was an expectation that she, as a student from an Indian family whose house "was the house where everybody came, and it was just big pots of Indian food to feed everybody," would shave the edges off her flavour profiles to satisfy what her instructors wanted to see as she made dishes like homemade mac and cheese and pie.

When I ask Maharaj if she has any food memories that stand out to her, of something she wouldn't necessarily have tasted if she didn't work in food, she immediately recalls a spoonful of olive oil she had in Italy. "I had been told here by Italian friends that the measure of good olive oil was something you could drink a spoonful of," she says. "And I had never tasted anything here that I was happy to drink a spoonful of." And then she went to Tuscany and taste-tested in an olive grove. "I was a different person after that," she says. The same thing happened with tomatoes, she says.

"It changed everything," Maharaj says. The Italians and the French, she adds, are no jokes when it comes to their food. They expect adherence to high standards.

It shows up through the whole system, she says. And they are able to maintain those standards because, unlike in North America, everyone in that whole system, from the people growing the food to the people cooking it and serving it, are valued.

This contrasts pretty starkly with the way most culinary workers are deeply undervalued in Canada and across North America. When I started working in the late 1990s, minimum wage for students under eighteen was $6.40 in Ontario. For everyone else, $6.85. One job paid me $5 an hour under the table. A couple of the places I worked paid a little bit more; those jobs emerged through word of mouth.

Two decades later, while wages look higher on paper, they're paltry in comparison to other industries and the current cost of living. The average wage in Canada in 2021, in today's dollars, was $30.67 an hour. In transportation and warehousing, $29.94. In educational services, $36.70. In agriculture, $20.78.

In accommodation and food services, the average wage was $17.34.

Meanwhile, in 2021, the living wage rate in Vancouver was $20.52 an hour; by 2023, it had increased to $25.68 an hour.

The hours for culinary work can be gruelling, and cooks often don't receive the rests and meal breaks they're legally entitled to. Kitchens are hot and moist, and cuts and burns are frequent. For people who like food and cooking, and care about their jobs, the satisfaction comes from serving meals that taste good and satiate your customers. To this end, cooks train their palates and noses to pick up on the small details—to tell the difference between nice vanilla extract and crappy vanilla extract, to balance the sweetness in a soup depending on the sweetness of the carrots that arrived in that week's produce order. They learn how to manipulate and understand things like heat. Through a lot of repetition and practice, they learn knife skills, consistency, and how things are supposed to feel as they stir them and they thicken, or sear them and they release.

Whatever affinity for food cooks enter a kitchen with, they increase assiduously in service of others. But most workers are paid so poorly that their jobs do not allow them to afford a meal at the very place they labour. At a mid-scale mom and pop restaurant where I live, pad Thai and a Diet Coke, with tax and tip, costs $23.49—one hour and twenty-one minutes of kitchen work paid at the average of $17.35 an hour. At a higher-end steakhouse in Vancouver, steak au poivre and a glass of pinot noir, with tax and tip, runs you $119.91—six hours and fifty-five minutes of kitchen work.

Growing up, most of the food my parents made was inexpensive, basic, quick to prepare, and aligned with my class status: peanut butter and banana on toast, beans on toast, frozen ravioli casserole, tuna casserole made with canned cream of mushroom soup, ham and scalloped potatoes, pasta sauce heated in a plastic measuring cup in the microwave and dolloped onto plain boiled noodles. Tim Hortons before early morning hockey practice. McDonald's on special occasions, or maybe a buffet if our grandparents were treating.

As a teen working in food service, I learned how to make Jean's salads and gained some knife skills; later, I learned to cook brunch, make a good soup, bake bread, make yogurt, mix and fry pakoras, bake date squares and butter tarts, mandolin radishes so thin they look like vellum. To make demi-glace, to nail the technique for Swiss meringue buttercream, because American buttercream is too sweet and tastes of anti-caking agent. To grow my own San Marzano tomatoes and use them to make Marcella Hazan's can't-be-improved-upon four-ingredient tomato sauce, which calls only for tomatoes, butter, onion, and salt.

In other words, working in kitchens led me to develop tastes I had no business developing. Even today, I dress like a person who balks at Value Village's recent price increases; I eat like a tenured humanities professor who purchased a home in Vancouver in 1994. I will not indebt myself to buy a car. I *will* indebt myself to buy one hundred grams each of all three of the semi-soft, raw milk, organic French cheeses the cheese shop carries so that I can compare them to see how they differ and decide which one I prefer. I *will* indebt myself when the stand mixer or enamelled cast iron pot I've been coveting goes on sale. I will fry my own gluten-free doughnuts because gluten-free doughnuts are best extremely fresh and still warm. I will buy myself a water-sealed fermentation crock for my birthday so I can more easily make fermented hot sauces and kimchi at home. When I visit the city, I will make a special trip to a specialty store in order to restock my favourite brand of smoked paprika. And when I watch the real estate and interior design shows on Netflix and HGTV— *Selling Sunset, Dream Home Makeover, Love It or List It*—or see nice kitchens in *Architectural Digest*, I will not covet their views or their custom sofas, but I will believe I deserve the kitchens rich people think they deserve.

It's not that food has to be expensive to be good. Or that it's impossible to make great food using humble tools. But fundamentally why should the person responsible for making something delicious not get to eat it? If it is my skill and palate creating the meal, I deserve to be able to eat that meal. And the people who will best make use of kitchen tools are the ones most deserving of owning them. Wealthy people get easy access to expensive food and tools; some of those wealthy people seek out that food and those tools because they like to eat and cook. But some seek out that food and those tools as markers of their wealth, cycling through brands and cuisines as if a well-built mixer, or an entire country's food culture, can go off-trend. And so to me, it's only fair that the working-class aesthetes and gluttons and grandmothers and farm workers driving those con-sumers' choices with their labour and creativity receive access too. Preferably by raising their wages and increasing access to affordable housing. But at minimum, by ensuring workers get a chance to sit for fifteen minutes in order to eat their own break-fast or lunch or dinner.

After I moved out and before I graduated and began working an ill-suited communications job, the free meal I ate at whatever kitchen job I was working was sometimes the only substantial food I ate that day. In 2004, Ontario's minimum wage increased to $7.15 an hour; by 2007, it reached $8. The push, at that time, was a $10 minimum wage—achieved far later than it was needed, with inflation outpacing wage gains. I spent these years in pov-erty, calculating in my head how many shift hours it would take to earn enough to pay rent, pay my bills, buy groceries. This sometimes led to a sense of futility: if I couldn't afford to replace my shoes, worn out from being on my feet for so many hours, I may as well spend what I'd earned that day on post-work beers at the Jimmy Jazz (still open) and a vegan burrito at the Salsateria (now closed, RIP). I thought I was terrible with money; when a friend who'd paid her tuition using a line of credit chose to pursue bankruptcy, I realized we were all just very underpaid.

Working in kitchens changed my relationship to food and my access to it, broadening my palate and allowing me to explore techniques, ingredients, and methods I wouldn't have been exposed to otherwise. It began with the delight of a cantaloupe and ended because it was so exhausting for such little pay, and the irony of being food-insecure while feeding others became too much to take.

"I just finished watching the movie *The Menu* again, to drink it in," Maharaj tells me. "It's a scathing indictment of fine dining culture, on both sides of the counter.

"Places like this, scenarios like this, have nothing to do with hunger. This is performance and art and status and conspicuous consumption. Do the cooks have to be able to eat that? This is not about four square meals a day, right? It's 1,250 dollars a plate."

But, Maharaj says, there's an inextricability connected to food that makes the gap between cooks' wages and the price of a meal seem worse, whatever the restaurant—because food, alongside shelter, air, and water, is a basic building block of survival. Culinary culture, Maharaj says, conditions chefs to believe that at the early juncture of their careers, they should be okay with poverty and starvation; this period represents the hardship before the chef gets to become "some sort of wild dictator" running their own kitchen. But despite what we may be indoctrinated to believe—and despite how far any given fine dining plate represents performance and art—there's something within us that finds this gap fundamentally unjust.

Maharaj contrasts the chafe of fine dining to her time working at The Stop Community Food Centre in Toronto, and the level of satisfaction she had in knowing her knowledge and labour were actually being helpful to people, participating in what she characterizes as a basic human connection. "My job is to highlight and underline the fact that we don't do anything that takes us too far away from meeting this very basic simple human need," Maharaj says. "Because it's food! I think it's reckless and irresponsible for us to let food become a thing that is this unattainable for people. It's fuckin' nuts. We should not have let it get this crazy."

Everyone deserves to have transformative moments eating food: ripe cantaloupe, fragrant olive oil, rich earthy chocolate, something fresh and salty from the ocean. Food should not be symbolic of the alienation of people from their labour and creativity; workers need to be paid enough, and cuisines need to be accessible enough, that cooks and farmers can meaningfully participate in the culture they create.

twenty-four batches
of ice cream

About two years ago, my friends Ben and Michael mailed me a chest-warming gift. I'd just had surgery to radically reduce the size of my chest, so that I could feel more at home in my non-binary body. The ice cream maker was the perfect gift, in the vein of teaching a man to fish: I could celebrate over and over again, testing out as many different kinds of ice cream as I wanted to. Ben and Michael own their own ice cream maker, and the gift reminded me of all the time I'd spent in their apartment, hanging out, sleeping over on their pull-out couch, taste-testing.

The first ice cream I churned, just a few weeks after my surgery in late January 2021, was Nutella flavoured—one of the sixteen flavours suggested as a "jumping-off point" by the *New York Times'* Master Ice Cream Recipe, published in summer 2014 and developed by Melissa Clark. I toasted some hazelnuts we had in the cupboard for a garnish, and started a spreadsheet to track the flavours I was testing, documenting flavour, date made, recipe source, and notes. "Yum," I wrote about the Nutella ice cream, and nothing further.

Next, I made a mediocre vegan chocolate ice cream using coconut milk. Notes: "Should be fuller fat." Then another deviation from a standard custard base: a *Serious Eats* recipe by Max

Falkowitz for strawberry ice cream, called "The Best Strawberry Ice Cream," that calls for keeping the strawberries fresh and macerating them in alcohol to preserve their bright spring flavour, uses half and half instead of heavy cream, and relies on the use of corn syrup to achieve a smooth texture free of ice crystals. This batch of ice cream, made using wild strawberries from our backyard, won the opinion of the household. "Very good," I wrote in my notes.

In the early summer, Will's goumi berry tree produced. Overconfident, I soaked pitted goumi berries in crème de cassis and sugar overnight, drained them, and mixed them, in a glass Tupperware, with a yuzu and lemon-flavoured ice cream base I'd made with yuzu zest from the freezer and a lemon from the grocery store. If you google goumi berries, you'll discover the tree from which they grow is a nitrogen fixer; you'll see the berries described as "tart" and "edible." You can read between the lines and guess what happened next. The yuzu-lemon base was impeccable—gentle and sweet; the goumi berries, rather than adding little hits of interest, were so astringent they stripped our tongues and inner cheeks of moisture upon contact.

A couple days after I made the ice cream, as I was trying to decide what I could do with it—if we'd get used to the very peculiar experience of the goumi berries, or if I should scoop them individually out of the ice cream in order to salvage it—I went to the freezer to pull out frozen corn while making dinner and caught the edge of the glass Tupperware housing the yuzu-lemon-goumi ice cream. It fell and smashed on the floor, which freed us from goumi purgatory but felt like a very big waste of heavy cream, eggs, yuzu zest, and expensive glass Tupperware.

Still, I wasn't too bothered; the ice cream maker was working as intended, as a tool for experimentation, joy, celebration. A way to satisfy our cravings and use harvests from our garden.

That summer, I got a call from my brother. He asked me where I was, if I was sitting down, if I was at home, or in public—the universal preamble for bad news. Our dad was having a heart attack, he said, and he'd just followed his ambulance to the hospital. COVID rules were in place and my brother wasn't allowed into the ER. He was calling from the hospital parking lot. Though I was 4,500 kilometres away, it felt like we were in the same boat. All we could do was wait and hope.

Eventually, my dad had an emergency angioplasty and received a stent. While in the hospital, he was also told he had diabetes. He came home—or, rather, went to my aunt and uncle's to convalesce—with a maraca set full of new medication and a very restrictive new diet.

One of the first things I thought about after I knew my dad was safe was the spreadsheet for my ice creams. And then I thought of my biological grandfather, Alan. We'd been estranged from him for years; he hadn't been around much for his family even when he'd been around on paper. We'd heard through the Ontario Hydro grapevine (he worked there, my aunt and uncle worked there, my brother works there) that he'd had a quadruple bypass sometime in the 2000s. Later, we heard he'd eventually died. Heart failure, we guessed. ("Ironic," someone said.)

Alan had fucked off, but in some ways we were all stuck with him. Had his last name, his tendency towards high blood pressure, high cholesterol, heart issues. As I worried about my dad, I wondered if I should abandon my ice cream making project. (Was it a project? The spreadsheet made it feel like a project.) Drafting the proposal to this book, I'd initially been thinking of this essay as "One Hundred Batches of Ice Cream." Upon reflection, maybe a hundred was an unwise goal.

There is a basic method for making most homemade ice cream bases: combine cream, milk, sugar, and flavourings in a heavy-bottomed pot. Whisk these ingredients together while bringing them to a simmer over medium heat. Meanwhile, crack some eggs, separating the yolks from the whites. Save the whites for a later purpose (like Swiss meringue buttercream or macarons or amaretti), and place the yolks in a medium-sized bowl. When the cream mixture begins to steam, take it off the heat, and slowly mix a third of it, or half of it, or all if you want to, into the yolks, whisking constantly. Once the warm cream mixture has been successfully integrated into the yolks, pour the whole thing back into the pot, continuing to whisk as if your wrists do not suffer from any repetitive stress injuries. Place the pot back on medium-low heat, and stir gently but consistently for five or six minutes. Over the course of this five or six minutes, the custard will reach a temperature of 170 degrees Fahrenheit and begin, almost imperceptibly, to thicken. When it's done, it'll be able to coat the back of a spoon. Now it's time to strain, bring to room temp, and chill. You can churn the ice cream once it's thoroughly refrigerated.

Each ice cream is slightly different. If you're making Kahlua-coffee, the flavourings go in with the cream and milk. If you're making Nutella, you whisk it into the warm custard after you've incorporated the egg yolks, thickened and strained.

But most ice cream involves the stovetop step—the alchemy of milk and cream and sugar and egg yolks turning into much more than the sum of their parts. I love eating ice cream, but maybe even more than eating it, I love to watch it come together on the stove, getting hot in service of, later, getting as cold as possible.

I am estranged from my mother and her family, as my dad was estranged from his father before him. I'm not necessarily great at keeping in touch even with the people I want to keep in touch with. So sometimes, when I think about the course of life, I think about how it involves an increasing series of losses and fractures. And it sounds ridiculous, but making custard offers a small opportunity to watch things coalesce, rather than fall apart. The threat of failure—the eggs scrambling, the custard breaking under too high a heat—is not so great as to provide frustration, but present enough that each success actually feels like a success. An edible, quick-turnaround success. Not one I wanted to give up.

After the "Best Strawberry Ice Cream" and the heart attack, I made a fuller-fat vegan chocolate coconut ice cream with gluten-free Oreos crushed and added in the last minute of churning. This was an improvement on the previous batch. Then Sinclair requested a peach and almond ice cream cake for her late-fall birthday. I sandwiched layers of almond cake around ice cream made from tinned peaches (the best bet, out of season), iced the cake with whipped cream, and covered the top in rainbow sprinkles.

Next, a Kahlua-coffee ice cream I used in a tiramisu baked Alaska, meant to mirror Richard's tiramisu baked Alaska from series five, episode four of *The Great British Bake Off*—somewhat infamously, the episode in which Iain's baked Alaska melts, and he bins it and presents the bin to the judges. (Notes: "SO GOOD.")

My dad slowly got better and looked more like himself. His favourite fish and chips shop, which he'd previously visited every Friday, closed during this period; he was well enough that we could joke that his lack of patronage had single-handedly put it out of business.

For Will's birthday, I made a watermelon bombe—pistachio ice cream for the green layer of the rind, store-bought coconut for the white layer, and raspberry ice cream studded with shards of gluten-free Oreo wafer for the juicy red fruit and pips. I placed a thin circular vanilla sponge on top of the bowl holding the ice cream, and then inverted it and removed a wedge, which looked pleasingly like a cartoon watermelon slice.

And then a mango coconut ice cream to use up some leftover mango purée: a scant two cups of purée, a can of coconut milk, some maple syrup, and some salt. A coffee base with mix-ins: Junior Mints, Reese's cups, Aero bits, Caramilk bits. (Notes: "Like having gotten stoned in the Ben & Jerry's test kitchen.")

In mid-May, and again in early June, for ice cream sandwiches, because it was popular, mint ice cream with David Lebovitz's recipe for fudge ripple.

I thought about conversations about mortality I used to have with my father as a child. What happened, I asked him, often, when a person died? He told me that some people believed in God, and that when you died, you went to some kind of afterlife. He said he personally did not believe in God or an afterlife. When that's it, that's it, he said. Believing the second scenario to be more likely, I kept pressing him, over years, for details. What *happened* then, I asked. Where did your *being* go? Back to the earth, my dad told me. To rejoin the earth and turn into something else. Nobody knew, really, about consciousness. That unknowing was ultimately the scaffolding of religion, he said. The goal of life was to learn how to live with the uncertainty, rather than trying to build a scaffolding for it.

When I was older, my father described being with his granddad Walter as he died. My father said it was like watching someone cling to life with every fibre of will he had and losing the battle. He said he, too, would cling to life, that he'd be dragged kicking and screaming to death while clinging to the cliff of the living with his fingertips.

For all this, however, my dad believes life is for living, for enjoying. He and I share a dopamine-seeking, celebratory approach to daily life, the basic belief that it is in these daily moments that we find meaning. It's a tension.

Around the anniversary of my dad's heart attack, I made one of my favourite flavours yet: spruce tip.

Spruce tip ice cream is less a tension and more a clear inter-mingling with our evergreen coastal surroundings. Christopher Cheung and I cowrote a piece for *The Tyee* in which he tested a Philadelphia-style base, and I called Kirsten Wood, a Cree ice cream maker and the owner of Blue Spruce Ice Cream, a small-batch shop located near the 5th Street Bridge in Courtenay, for tips on how best to infuse my classic custard-style base with spruce tips collected from the blue spruce in my yard. Wood told me that for her, making spruce tip ice cream is, in part, an expression of the relationship between Indigenous approaches to food and locally available ingredients. With her suggestions, I made an ice cream that was so good I plan to make it yearly as long as our blue spruce is standing and I can harvest from it.

Later that same summer, I made what I have taken to calling my life's work. I'm not sure what sparked it, but I began to won-der if the Momofuku Cereal Milk ice cream technique could be applied to pretzels—specifically gluten-free pretzels. It was a two-day ordeal: caramelizing crushed gluten-free pretzels in sugar and dry milk powder in the oven, and steeping them in four cups of whole-fat milk in order to make *one* cup of pretzel-infused milk. From there, making the custard, and churning the custard.

Initially, my plan was to make chocolate-covered pretzels to add as a mix-in; it was rich enough without—the salty, toasty-bread flavour of the pretzels needed to be enjoyed on its own.

Will thought the pretzel flavour was an abomination. This was good news for me, because I did not want to share.

After the pretzel ice cream, a disappointing chalky vegan lemon ice cream. And then a plum ice cream made using a jar of plums my friend Erin had canned. The resulting ice cream was rich and a bit salty. I used much of it to make a frozen meringue pie with a graham crumb base and a toasted meringue top.

Then I made a peanut butter ice cream and placed the leftover plum alongside the peanut butter ice cream in silicone ice cream bar moulds to make PB&J ice cream bars. (Buying the moulds felt like acquiring a new superpower. Ice cream in a bowl is one thing; ice cream on sticks, dipped into milk or white or dark chocolate, and then rolled in toasted nuts or sprinkles, is a whole new thing entirely.)

And then a satsuma ice cream, used in mini baked Alaskas with a brownie base, and an orange sherbet, because the satsuma ice cream was subtle and I wanted to know if I could make something that tasted juicy.

Nutella ice cream again ("cannot be improved upon"), and a yuzu encore, this time with no goumi berries. And then blackberry.

Finally, in March 2023, just over two years after I started the project, s'mores. I made a chocolate base, toasted the mini marshmallow mix-ins with a culinary torch, and enrobed gluten-free graham crackers in chocolate so they'd remain crunchy.

My friend Jen shared the s'mores ice cream with her best friend Jenn, who's celiac, while they were house-sitting for Will and Sinclair and me—we were in Vancouver for my nephew's birthday. In the middle of painting an overturned half-dome cake so that it would look like Jupiter, my nephew's favourite planet, I got a text from Jen: a photo of Jenn's face halfway into a ceramic bowl, licking it clean—"How Jenn feels about the ice cream."

One of the things I wonder about, with my dad and mortality, is whether he has, in part, lived his life as a rebellion against the self-denial and moderation preached by the Methodist church of his youth. Why go to all the trouble of parting from it to opt back in for health reasons? Why reach ninety if reaching ninety means no whiskey or fish and chips or weed gummies? From his initial, fairly strict, recovery diet, he's branched back out into a more varied diet that includes more of the foods he actually enjoys eating. Another tension that emerges is that I don't believe we owe health to anyone—but I do want to harangue my father as if I am his dietitian or fitness coach, because his heart attack was terrifying and I would like to see him grow old.

While I do find pleasure in places other than food—swimming in the ocean, walking around new places, making art, seeing art, reading books, rewatching familiar TV series—food is a joy that reaches out as a daily necessity, regular and accessible. In the end, I scaled back my initial goal of reaching one hundred batches of ice cream in two years, churning twenty-four in just over two years instead. But like my nana and my Grandma Garcia and my dad, I generally eat a bit of dessert, a little something sweet, ice cream or not, every day. Is this moderation? Is this healthy? Health is holistic. Moderation is subjective.

I do feel plagued, sometimes, by my family history and by the statistics that say as a trans person and a person with bipolar disorder, I will live a shorter life than my peers. I want to live forever. Literally forever. But this feeling lifts when I cook and bake things that I enjoy and can share with others. When I engage in the practical creativity that food represents. I haven't resolved the essential tension, or the essential question; in fact it's difficult to disentangle in a culture saturated with fatphobia and shifting trends and ideas about what exactly leads to and constitutes health and wellness. Standing over the stove watching the custard come together, it's less that I resolve the essential tension between ideas of health and pleasure—or even if there *is* an essential tension— than that I forget about it for a time. And maybe that's enough.

SPRUCE TIP ICE CREAM

Conifer tips emerge in the spring, bright green and soft, wrapped in papery, sticky sheaths at the end of each branch. You'll need to harvest a generous cup for this recipe. I suggest doing some googling and reading up on spruce identification before going in search of some mature trees. Spruce can look very similar to fir, for example, but you can tell them apart by examining their needles—flat needles mean fir, and four-sided needles that roll easily between your fingers signify spruce. Spruce is pretty easy to spot, but it's important to feel comfortable and confident before harvesting. Some confers, like yew, are poisonous and need to be avoided.

This recipe will take about two days total to complete, as you'll want to steep the spruce tips in the custard for thirty-six to forty-eight hours.

TOOLS

- whisk
- medium-sized heavy-bottomed pot

- medium-sized fine-mesh strainer
- food thermometer (optional but helpful)
- ice cream maker (optional but helpful)

INGREDIENTS

- 2 cups heavy cream
- 1 cup milk
- ⅔ cup sugar
- generous pinch of salt
- 6 egg yolks (save the whites for another use; I often freeze them)
- ¼ cup lemon juice
- 1 cup spruce tips

1. Place the six egg yolks into a mixing bowl. Whisk them together and set aside.
2. Whisk the cream, milk, sugar, and salt together in a medium-sized heavy-bottomed pot on medium-low heat until the sugar has dissolved and the mixture is beginning to emit the tiniest bit of steam.
3. Take the pot off the heat.
4. Slowly drizzle about one-third of the hot cream mixture into the egg yolks, whisking constantly. The idea is to temper the yolks, which keeps them from scrambling.
5. Once you've added one-third of the cream mixture into the yolks, it's time to add that yolk mixture back into the main pot. Keeping the pot off the heat, slowly drizzle the yolk mixture back into the cream mixture, whisking constantly.
6. Place the pot back onto a medium-low heat and gently cook the custard, whisking regularly. You're looking for the custard to come to 170°F (77°C). If

you don't have a thermometer, it should be thick enough to coat the back of a spoon.

7. Remove the pot from the heat and let it come to room temperature for half an hour on the countertop.

8. Meanwhile, wash and dry your spruce tips, and roughly chop them into largeish pieces.

9. After a half hour, stir the lemon juice and your spruce tips into the custard base.

10. Transfer into a bowl and place in the fridge. (Or just place the pot into the fridge; we're not judging.)

11. Allow the spruce tips to infuse into the custard in the fridge for 36 to 48 hours.

12. Strain the custard through a fine-mesh strainer into a new bowl. It's okay if a few little spruce bits make it through.

13. Churn the ice cream in your ice cream maker, or DIY using a baking pan and a whisk.

14. Serve in a cup or cone.

PRETZEL-INFUSED ICE CREAM

Adapted from the Momofuku recipe for Cereal Milk ice cream

TOOLS

- baking sheet
- parchment paper
- whisk
- medium-sized heavy-bottomed pot
- medium-sized fine-mesh strainer
- food thermometer (optional but helpful)
- ice cream maker (optional but helpful)

INGREDIENTS

For caramelized pretzels

- 280 grams (10 ounces) pretzels (or gluten-free pretzels)
- 55 grams (2 ounces) dry milk powder
- 4 tablespoons sugar
- 185 grams (6.5 ounces) unsalted butter, melted

For pretzel-infused milk

- 4 cups whole milk
- caramelized pretzels

For pretzel-infused ice cream (makes approximately 3.5 cups)

- 1 cup heavy cream
- 1 cup pretzel-infused milk
- 1/2 cup (100 grams) sugar
- 1/4 teaspoon salt
- 1 teaspoon vanilla extract
- 4 large egg yolks
- a handful of crushed pretzels, to serve

To caramelize pretzels

1. Preheat your oven to 275°F (135°C). Put the pretzels in a food processor, blender, or clean mortar and pestle to reduce them to pea-sized or smaller pieces.
2. Combine milk powder and sugar in another bowl. Stir. Add the melted butter. Stir. Add the crushed pretzels and mix well.
3. Spread the mixture onto a baking sheet lined with

parchment paper, and bake until the crushed pretzels caramelize, approximately 35 minutes. Remove and let cool to room temperature.

To make pretzel-infused milk

1. Combine the caramelized pretzels and milk in a large mixing bowl and let steep for an hour. Strain the milk through a fine-mesh sieve, squeezing the pretzels to extract the milk. Clean the strainer. Strain again into a clean bowl; this time, don't press or squeeze anything.

To make pretzel-infused ice cream

1. Pour the heavy cream into a medium bowl and place it in the fridge.
2. Combine the pretzel-infused milk, sugar, salt, and vanilla extract in a small pot and heat over medium-low until the mixture begins to steam.
3. In the meantime, in a medium-sized mixing bowl, whisk together the egg yolks. Slowly pour the warm milk mixture into the yolks while whisking constantly. Place over medium heat and stir until the custard comes to 170°F (77°C). If you don't have a thermometer, it should be thick enough to coat the back of a spoon.
4. Pour the custard through a strainer into the chilled heavy cream and stir to combine.
5. Chill the mixture overnight, then churn your ice cream base in your ice cream maker. Or DIY using a baking pan and a whisk.
6. Serve with some crushed pretzels as a garnish.

S'MORES ICE CREAM

Base adapted from the *New York Times*
Master Ice Cream Recipe by Melissa Clark

It's easiest to make this ice cream over two days. On day one, make the base and enrobe the graham crackers in melted chocolate. On day two, torch the mini marshmallows, break the chocolate-covered graham crackers apart on the Silpat, churn the ice cream, and mix everything together.

TOOLS

- Silpat
- culinary torch
- whisk
- small mixing bowl
- medium-sized mixing bowl
- large mixing bowl
- medium-sized heavy-bottomed pot
- medium-sized fine-mesh strainer
- food thermometer (optional but helpful)
- ice cream maker (optional but helpful)

INGREDIENTS

Ice cream base

- 170 grams (6 ounces) semi-sweet Baker's chocolate
- 3 tablespoons cocoa powder
- 1 ½ cups whole milk
- ¾ cup sugar
- pinch of salt
- 6 egg yolks

- ¾ cup sour cream
- 1 teaspoon vanilla extract

Mix-ins

- 200 grams (7 ounces) mini marshmallows
- 100 grams (3.5 ounces) graham crackers (if using gluten-free, I recommend the Schär gluten-free Honeygrams)
- 170 grams (6 ounces) Baker's chocolate

1. Chop finely, or shave, the semi-sweet baking chocolate into a small mixing bowl.
2. In a medium-sized heavy-bottomed pot, bring the cream and cocoa powder to a simmer, stirring. When it's hot, pour it over the chocolate, place a clean tea towel over the bowl, and set it aside.
3. Place six egg yolks into a medium-sized mixing bowl. Whisk them together and set aside.
4. Clean out the pot. Whisk the milk, sugar, and salt together in the pot on medium-low heat until the sugar has dissolved and the mixture is beginning to steam. Take the pot off the heat.
5. Slowly drizzle about one-third of the hot cream mixture into the egg yolks, whisking constantly.
6. Add that yolk mixture back into the main pot. Keeping the pot off the heat, slowly drizzle the yolk mixture back into the cream mixture, whisking constantly.
7. Place the pot back onto a medium-low heat and gently cook the custard, whisking regularly. You're looking for the custard to come to 170°F (77°C). If you don't have a thermometer, it should be thick enough to coat the back of a spoon.

8. Strain the custard through the fine-mesh sieve into a clean mixing bowl. (I usually quickly wash out the one that was housing my yolks.) Whisk in the melted chocolate mixture, as well as ¾ cup of sour cream. Add your teaspoon of vanilla.

9. Let the base come to room temperature for half an hour on the countertop. Then place it in the fridge. Allow it to chill for at least four hours. (I usually leave mine overnight.)

10. Meanwhile, work on enrobing your graham crackers in chocolate. Set out a Silpat (or parchment paper). Break the graham crackers into bite-sized pieces. Chop the chocolate and place it into a microwave-safe bowl. Microwave it in thirty-second increments, stirring in between each session, until it's fully melted—about two or three sessions. Add the graham cracker pieces to the melted chocolate, and gently fold together with a spatula until the graham crackers are coated in chocolate. Overturn the chocolate-coated graham crackers onto the Silpat and spread them out so they'll be easy to snap apart when they've solidified in a few hours. I cover mine with a baking sheet (you could also put them in Tupperware) and leave them out at room temperature overnight.

11. The next day (or when your base is chilled and your enrobed graham crackers have solidified), lay the marshmallows out in a flat layer on a platter—something that isn't terribly melty or flammable. Using a culinary torch, toast the marshmallows until they have golden-brown and burnt bits. Set aside.

12. Churn your ice cream base in your ice cream maker. Or DIY using a baking pan and a whisk.

13. Your mix-ins will *not* fit into a regular-sized ice cream maker. When the ice cream is done churning, scoop it into a large bowl, layering it with the graham cracker and marshmallow mix-ins (making sure to add only bite-sized chunks of marshmallow at a time—if you add a big chunk, it might freeze into a big clump!). Mix together gently using a wooden spoon. Working quickly, scoop it into your container of choice (mine fit roughly into two large-size Adams peanut butter jars) and place it into the freezer for a few hours to solidify before serving.

pestilence and abundance

There are lessons to be learned in the mindful, long-term care of plants. My partner, Will, has kept dozens of indoor plants alive for the entire time I've known him. These plants—euphorbias and cacti, ferns and broadleaf evergreens—get all manner of pests I most likely never would have heard of if it wasn't for meeting him. Thrips, mealies, root mealies, spider mites—Will kills them all. He checks in on his plants diligently, watering them and repotting them, pruning and root pruning them. The bigger plants, he waters in the bathtub. The pots of oxalis, which grow from corms, get periodic haircuts. Why? He's explained it to me, but I'm never quite sure. At regular intervals throughout the week, he moves through the house with a watering can, a repurposed toaster oven grill, and a bucket to catch the excess water. Anything that needs a soak is set on the grill over the bucket and tended to with indoor artificial rain.

Will has written about taking care of these plants, saying that he finds something thrilling about keeping them all alive—that they lend a purpose to his life, especially if they originated in an illicit roadside cutting or involved an illegal border crossing. I think this kind of care must also be somewhat meditative—slowing the world down, focusing on long-term, persistent solutions to pests and problems.

But there's also satisfaction in helping an annual or biennial vegetable mope along until it crops.

Many permaculturalists and regenerative farmer types and backyard gardeners into no-till farming—which, for the uninitiated, means top-dressing garden beds or fields with compost or aged manure annually, rather than digging it in or using fertilizers—will tell you that if your farm or garden is diverse and in balance, you will not see significant pest or disease pressure.

Over time, in broad strokes, this is true: practising crop rotation can help guard against or suppress some pathogens, in addition to improving soil quality by, for example, planting nitrogen fixers such as peas and beans following a year spent growing brassicas, such as broccoli and Brussels sprouts, which draw heavily on nitrogen stores. Diversity can also help attract beneficial insects and pollinators, and it helps ensure a yield even in years that are overly hot or cold or rainy or dry, if varieties with different strengths and weaknesses have been planted. But it's also true that things are just sometimes a crapshoot.

The first year we moved into our house, as soon as the soil in the backyard was workable, we began to dig out the sod and create garden beds. First with a handsaw and then with a chainsaw, Will removed a row of cedar hedges from the south side of the backyard to let in more light. He trimmed back the overgrown laurel hedge, which was so tall it arched over the asphalt tile roof of our house, creating issues with water, moss, and leaf detritus. He cut back a dead hazelnut tree; he pruned and snipped and eventually there grew large piles of neatly organized shrub and tree trimmings. Not all of them were suitable for our purposes, but we used what we could in the newly dug-out beds, layering trimmings with sod underneath soil we'd dug out from further down.

This first year, we managed to create three long north-south beds—one that would act as a nursery for the young trees and shrubs Will propagated, and two for my vegetables. We left grass between the beds and lined them with laurel limbs. They looked nice: tidy, fresh, cared for. Our cat, Mackerel, on a harness and sunning herself on the deck, watched over our progress. I bought her cat grass, repotting a tightly bound clump into three separate containers.

I started simple that year, growing peppers, tomatoes, kale, peas, beans, broccoli, and favas. I tried to seed carrots, but they didn't germinate. We started the tomatoes, peppers, and broccoli inside the house, letting the seedlings grow strong before transplanting them out. I seeded the peas and kale directly in the soil.

Soon I discovered a problem: the damp, mostly grassy habitat of the yard was absolutely perfect for slugs, and in turning over the sod to create garden beds, and then lining those beds with small logs, we'd created a perfect little slug bed and breakfast. They ate large holes in the brassica leaves; they felled peas and tomatoes. They were everywhere, like a Biblical plague. Under the grape arbour, there was a U-shaped set of beds with concrete walls where I planted herbs. I was particularly invested in the basil. So were the slugs.

I tried suggested remedies, like spreading coffee grounds and eggshells, but they didn't work. A German-language website I found went into depth trialling "anti-schnecken" techniques—placing snails and slugs in little experiments to see what worked as a deterrent. The creatures' protective mucus allowed them to glide over anything poky with ease. Three things worked: wide copper tape, a somewhat complicated physical barrier known as a slug fence, and literally shocking the slugs with bands of electrical wiring.

None of these options was immediately possible in my garden, so I began a war. At night I went outside wearing a headlamp and carrying a bucket of salt water, which I later traded in for scissors—less suffering, a more immediate death. I caught little grey field slugs in the act of snacking and felling and doled out immediate capital punishment. I killed dozens every night.

Soon I began to dream of the slugs. It felt a bit untenable. I became convinced that when I died, I'd have to meet them again and answer to each and every one that I'd killed.

I told everyone I met about the slugs. When they suggested folk remedies, I went into detail about the results of the anti-schnecken trials. Meanwhile, Will continued his dutiful attentions to his plants, not making their plagues anyone else's problem.

Near the end of the season, I realized that the logs we'd used to line the garden beds had to go. Will and I biked, with Sinclair in her baby bike seat and me hauling a bike trailer, to a set of cardboard dumpsters behind the dollar store and the Mark's Work Wearhouse in our town. Sinclair toddled around as Will climbed into the dumpster and frisbeed nice big uncoated boxes out towards me. We used the cardboard to smother the grass paths and heaped it high with wood chips—just sixty-five dollars for a load from a local arborist, which saved him a trip to the dump.

I still direct-seed very little—it helps the plants to let them grow large in their cells in the warmth of the hoop house (built in year two) or the greenhouse (built in year three). I grow my basil in five-gallon pots ringed with copper tape, and I wrap the tender stalks of my squash, cucumber, and melon seedlings with aluminum foil collars when I plant them out to keep them from being felled. But I no longer go out on nightly slug raids or see them in my dreams, my conscience haunting me.

In this case, the advice I'd been absorbing from hippieish experts panned out: the more we built up the soil and transitioned the grass to garden and wood chip paths, the less the slugs were a problem.

But it wasn't our last pestilence. And not all of them are solvable with habitat changes and patience. Some of them—especially as climate change renders each season a little weirder, a little less predictable—we just have to learn to live with, like we have to learn to live with grief or loss or the guilt of an unfixable trespass against a loved one.

The second year of the garden, I decided to let one of my overwintered curly kale plants, which had done quite well, go to seed. It doubled and then tripled in size before developing hundreds of stalks of small yellow flowers. (These were popular with bees and other flying insects, so much so that in the height of its bloom, the plant appeared to audibly hum.) We harvested some of the flowers and ate them; others soon turned into long thin pods, which I'd need to let dry out on the plant.

All was going well until it wasn't. I went out one afternoon to attend to something else—watering or weeding, or maybe harvesting some greens or purple sprouting broccoli—and realized that, seemingly overnight, the kale plant pods had been colonized by thousands of aphids. The plant was also alive with ants, which had most likely installed the aphids on the pods in order to farm the liquid they secrete, which is called honeydew and which ants love. The result was that the kale plant looked almost like coral. To me, it felt like I'd accidentally chosen the wrong movie on Netflix and found myself in medias res in some kind of body horror. I then realized the aphids were everywhere; I even discovered them on Mackerel's cat grass.

I'd already begun to reflect on the amount of death I'd meted out in order to see my fruit and vegetable plants through to harvest, and I had decided that gardening and farming, even when done organically with nothing approaching terminator seeds, pesticides, or herbicides, was not simply a life-giving act, an uncomplicated idyll. This I found almost funny: our garden, which we'd designed to feel like a bit of an oasis and which was one for many species of birds and pollinators, was the place where I was a backyard grim reaper.

I used the hose nozzle to send a hard spray of water to wash the aphids off the kale pods and then used my bare hands to crush the small bodies of the survivors, which so angered the ants— of course it did!—they began to swarm towards my fingers and palms and wrists and forearms to bite me.

For days and weeks, I fought off the ants and aphids, and they fought me. The kale plant would be temporarily clear and then begin to look like a terribly creepy land coral again. It was frustrating. I am sure my neighbours must have seen me stalk outside in rubber boots and boxers, cursing at insects and the sky.

In the end, I had to abandon parts of the plant. But the goal was to save seeds. And I did. I saved hundreds—enough to grow as many kale plants as I wanted for years, and to share with anyone who wanted curly kale. Abundance!

In year two of the garden, my carrots germinated, but when I picked them, I found many tunnelled through—little miniature tunnels caused by something called the carrot rust fly. The following year, I bought sheets of mesh from the gardening store, PVC piping from a local plumbing shop, and had eighteen-inch lengths of rebar cut at the Rona. I hammered the rebar into the soil, sawed lengths of piping, and curved little inverted Us that helped the mesh arch over the garden beds. Covering the carrots worked well to keep off carrot rust fly; covering the brassicas deterred cabbage moths and aphids.

In the cool damp of the Pacific Northwest, I discovered that growing my winter squash up trellises helped stave off the development of powdery mildew; it kept the fruits from developing soft or mouldy spots where they touched the ground and discouraged slugs from trying to latch onto the rind.

Pruning, or side shooting, the indeterminate tomatoes, removing lower leaves as they grow, keeping them the recommended distances away from each other, and staking them with T-posts, wire, bamboo, and cotton twine helped prevent funguses and blights by increasing air flow, and keeping everything neat and tidy meant that an affected plant could be yoinked before it passed its illness on.

Still, none of this is foolproof. The powdery mildew eventually takes over, and the squash vines look progressively less spry and healthy as their fruits crawl over the finish line of ripeness in mid-October. Some years, the tomatoes do so well, starting to ripen in July and going till November, that we tire of processing them and yearn for the winter. Other years, it's hot in May and cold in June and the first fruits to set have blossom end rot, or everyone in the area gets August or September blight and the fruits need to be picked green to pickle or ripen indoors.

Our season and microclimate also affect what grows well in our yard. I tried sui choy several times before realizing it would forever be destined to bolt here—nearing the fiftieth parallel, there isn't enough light in the early spring, and by May, when the days are long enough to promote lots of growth, it's too hot, and sensitive plants send up premature flower stalks. (The slugs also feasted on it.) When I grew my first successful cabbage varieties—deadon, which is purplish and mildly frilly, and Charmant, which is dense and smooth and green—I felt overjoyed. Neither would work in kimchi, which is what I wanted the sui choy for, but they'd work in other things, and more importantly, they'd work in the garden.

Last year was a mediocre year for broccoli, and such a great year for cucumbers that I struggled to keep up with harvesting them and gave dozens away, including to a local food security project after I'd exhausted my friends and neighbours. As I began this year's seedlings in March, and prepared this year's beds and garden infrastructure, we were still eating produce I processed and froze last summer and fall.

It feels a bit like chaos, but it's of course instead a complicated dance of factors, some—like watering and covering—I control, and others—like temperature and humidity and insect-borne illness—I don't. The truth is, I'm a perfectionist but one without Will's steady patience. Gardening has taught me about the pleasures of delayed gratification, and it's also taught me to accept that some things lie beyond my sphere of influence, and some things I'll never place *into* my sphere of influence, so long as Will is willing to tend to our fruit trees and citrus trees and shrubs.

Will has a never-ending list of tasks, one that is perennial, with the rhythms on a larger timescale. To keep our citrus trees happy in their pots, for example, he has to remove them every two or three years, prune their roots, and place them in fresh soil. This must be done when the trees are dormant. He often does this during a time of year when, exhausted from the harvest, I'm spending less time in the garden than I am playing *Stardew Valley*. Inside the house, it's more important to suppress any bugs that arrive, rather than simply manage them—an infestation of fungus gnats is as unpleasant for us as it is for the ficus or the coffee plant.

Outside, in the vegetable garden, the timescale for my annuals and biennials is more concentrated. They live, they produce, they die. It's unreasonable to want to kill off every insect that affects the plants. And as long as we're still able to harvest enough tomatoes for sauce, enough carrots to keep us going, it's not the end of the world to co-exist with slugs, aphids, even cabbage moths.

My plants do not look as perfect as those of my favourite no-till gardener, Charles Dowding. I look away for what feels like five minutes and creeping buttercup and bindweed have burst through my garden beds and found purchase, disrupting my carrots or winding around my gai lan. I neglect to remove the lower yellow-ing leaves from my broccoli, or kale, which I should have harvested sooner. The neighbour's oak sends acorns raining down all winter, and I discover their seedings in my peas, beans, strawberry bed. I think a cabbage looks beautiful, perfect, ready for Instagram; I remove the outer leaves and discover a slug has burrowed in and eaten a large hole, leaving its slimy castings as a bonus surprise.

But really, it's okay. It's okay that my produce is sometimes imperfect. It's still usable, even if it wouldn't be saleable at a grocery store, or would be deemed seconds by the farmers who harvest the vegetables that go into my CSA box. The fact that I've grown it, from seed to seedling to plant to harvest (and sometimes back to seed again), makes me more invested in salvaging it. I'm also more likely to use parts of a plant, like broccoli leaves, that are edible but not generally sold at the store. Why waste free greens?

Some years my favourite varieties aren't available, and what is available, and what I grow, is not as good as a result. As hybrids tailored to our shorter growing season, Halona melons, for exam-ple, crop faster than other kinds of cantaloupes, which take too long to mature. During peak COVID, Halona seeds weren't available; the other variety I grew matured in October, grumpily and without much flavour.

The garden offers bespoke lessons. Most of us are aiming for the same goal—grow food—using similar tools: seeds, soil. Beyond that, our particular microclimates, the slopes of our terrain, the surrounding flora and fauna all mean we face slightly different puzzles and are given slightly different opportunities. I can't grow sui choy and I don't like growing bulbing onions, but I can grow peppers and eggplants in my greenhouse, which might be trickier for someone who's not on a sunny plot right near a particularly shielded patch of the Pacific. That's what bartering and sharing are for.

Similarly, I come to gardening hoping it might perhaps solve my life by teaching me to understand patience and my place in the world. A tall order. Maybe, for someone like me, lifelong lessons stick each year about as well as latex paint adheres to oil-based paint. But a real lesson I have learned more resolutely, if painfully, is that it's okay to do my best and not be perfect, not excel, not patiently annihilate every single pest. Maybe a percentage of my crops each year will be great and another percentage will suffer subpar conditions, resulting in a mediocre harvest. What's mediocre is still edible. And there's often a cost to excellence. Sometimes, for the sake of happiness, excellence isn't worth it. Save the effort of an uprising for political goals; at home, in the garden, embrace periodic mediocrity.

The garden teaches gratefulness through its bounty and through its funguses, its aphids, its bolted cabbages. Every summer, it provides. It provides carrots and potatoes, peppers and garlic, saffron and basil and thyme, tomatoes, broccoli, squash, cucumber, zucchini, cantaloupe, celery, strawberries, blueberries. Even when it fails, it provides. Abundance, nourishment; a mediocre crop acting as a foil to last year's, or next year's, much better crop; sore muscles, warm sun, a cool breeze from the ocean. Provision.

acknowledgements

A previous version of "Tomato chutney, part I: reviving my nana's recipe" was published by *Chatelaine* as "Thicker Than Water." Thank you to Chantal Braganza for her insightful edits. Previous versions of "The garden will bloom again" and "Because someone saved the seed" were published by *The Tyee*, as were the kale pesto and spruce tip ice cream recipes.

The writing of this book was supported by a grant from the Canada Council for the Arts.

A very hearty thank you to everyone I spoke with and visited and farmed with and cooked with and ate with over the making of this book.

Thank you, as well, to my colleagues at *The Tyee*, in particular Christopher Cheung. To my incredibly supportive and talented editor, the dream editor for this book, Jen Knoch. And to Kim Fu, my best friend and favourite person in the whole world to discuss food with. And as always to my partner, Will, for helping me make the space to research and write. And for doing the vast majority of the dishes (by hand! Someday we'll get a dishwasher).

endnotes

ILLNESS AND APPETITE

"a persistent irritant to any chef worth a damn": Anthony
 Bourdain, *Kitchen Confidential: Adventures in the Culinary
 Underbelly* (New York: Bloomsbury, 2019), 78.

"teach youth about farming and our responsibility to the
 land": "Cane Creek Farm," Cane Creek Stewardship
 Camp, accessed January 17, 2024, https://canecreekfarm.us
 /cane-creek-stewardship-camp/.

"steamed broccoli is 'the root of all evil'": Jeffrey Steingarten,
 "Where's the *Boeuf?*" in *It Must Have Been Something I Ate*
 (New York: Vintage, 2002).

"he also writes approvingly about visiting Alain Passard's
 Arpège": Ryan Sutton, "The Crushing Disappointment of
 L'Arpège," *Eater*, October 19, 2016, https://www.eater.com
 /2016/10/19/13322232/paris-larpege-alain-passard-vegetables.

"I am dismissive and sometimes contemptuous of food": Aparna
 Pednekar, "What Anthony Bourdain Thinks about Indian
 food," *Vogue India*, May 11, 2017, https://www.vogue.in/content
 /what-anthony-bourdain-thinks-about-indian-food.

"a type of chronic gastritis that is 'strongly associated' with celiac
 disease": B. Lebwohl, P.H.R. Green, and R.M. Genta, "The

Coeliac Stomach: Gastritis in Patients with Coeliac Disease," *Alimentary Pharmacology and Therapeutics* 2, no. 2 (July 2015): 180–187, https://doi.org/10.1111/apt.13249.

"Per-capita meat consumption in the U.S.": M. Shahbandeh, "Per Capita Meat Consumption in the United States in 2022 and 2031, by Type," Statista, October 30, 2023, https://www.statista.com/statistics/189222/average-meat-consumption-in-the-us-by-sort/.

TWO BAGS OF LETTUCE

"Yuma, Arizona—one of the sunniest places in the world": Liz Osborn, "Sunniest Places and Countries in the World," Current Results, accessed January 17, 2024, https://www.currentresults.com/Weather-Extremes/sunniest-places-countries-world.php.

"oil and gas are running out": Gioietta Kuo, "When Fossil Fuels Run Out, What Then?" Millennium Alliance for Humanity and the Biosphere, May 2019, https://mahb.stanford.edu/library-item/fossil-fuels-run/.

"we're facing fertilizer shortages": Shea Swensen, "The Fertilizer Shortage Will Persist in 2023," *Modern Farmer*, December 1, 2022, https://modernfarmer.com/2022/12/the-fertilizer-shortage-will-persist-in-2023.

U.S. agricultural greenhouse gas emissions: U.S. Department of Agriculture Economic Research Service, "Climate Change," accessed January 17, 2023, https://www.ers.usda.gov/topics/natural-resources-environment/climate-change.

Canadian agricultural greenhouse gas emissions: Government of Canada, "Greenhouse Gas Emissions and Agriculture," accessed January 17, 2023, https://agriculture.canada.ca/en/environment/greenhouse-gases.

"agricultural employers are often cited for not following legally

mandated rest breaks and for wage theft": Department
of Industrial Relations Labor Enforcement Task Force,
"Protect Your Business—Prevent Penalties," 2022, https://
www.dir.ca.gov/letf/Agriculture_Employer_Brochure.pdf.

"heavily polluted Salton Sea in 1905": Dan Charles, "Meet the
California Farmers Awash in Colorado River Water, Even
in a Drought," NPR, October 4, 2022, https://www.npr.org
/2022/10/04/1126240060/meet-the-california-farmers-awash
-in-colorado-river-water-even-in-a-drought.

"delivering water to Imperial Valley in 1940": Imperial Irrigation
District, "All-American Canal," accessed January 17, 2024,
https://www.iid.com/water/water-transportation-system
/colorado-river-facilities/all-american-canal.

"the sole source of water to the area since 1942": Imperial
Irrigation District.

"their senior water rights mean they're legally entitled to do so":
Alastair Bland, "Growers Brace to Give Up Some Colorado
River Water," Cal Matters, January 17, 2023, https://calmatters
.org/environment/2023/01/colorado-river-water.

"they need to give up 10 percent of their supply": Bland, "Growers
Brace."

"most likely sown in late October or early November": Richard
Smith et al., Leaf Lettuce Production in California, University
of California Agriculture and Natural Resources. Publication
7216 (2011), https://anrcatalog.ucanr.edu/pdf/7216.pdf.

"the average farm in California covers about 351 acres": California
Department of Food and Agriculture, California Agricultural
Statistics Review. 2021–2022, https://www.cdfa.ca.gov/Statistics
/PDFs/2022_Ag_Stats_Review.pdf.

"the lettuces are usually watered by sprinklers for the first five
to seven days": Smith et al., Leaf Lettuce.

"it usually takes about three acre-feet, or 3,700 cubic metres, of
water per acre to grow leaf lettuce": Louise Jackson et al.,

Leaf Lettuce Production in California, University of California
Agriculture and Natural Resources, https://ucanr.edu
/repository/fileaccess.cfm?article=54025&p=%20QGYEXN.
"farmers often use the savings to increase their irrigated crop
area or grow more water-intensive produce": Marcia
MacNeil, "Overcoming the 'Paradox' of Irrigation Efficiency,"
International Food Policy Research Institute, November 8,
2018, https://www.ifpri.org/blog/overcoming-%E2%80%9
Cparadox%E2%80%9D-irrigation-efficiency-0.
"as much as 250 pounds per acre of phosphorus pre-planting, and
between 200 and 250 pounds per acre of nitrogen": Smith et
al., *Leaf Lettuce.*
"conventional pesticides are sprayed": Smith et al., *Leaf Lettuce.*
"It's chilly in the morning, about 9 degrees Celsius, and cloudy":
Imperial, CA, Weather History. Wunderground.com, March 1,
2023, https://www.wunderground.com/history/daily/mx/tecate
/KIPL/date/2023-3-1.
"Packers tape the bags closed": Chore Vlogs, "Corte de lechuga
de bola| así se gana el dinero trabajando," April 26, 2022,
https://youtu.be/hio3DbUlero.
"The speed of those guys is impressive": David T., "Corte de
lechuga (impresionante velocidad)," October 26, 2020, https://
youtu.be/lvT3sKzVwnc.
"We work in different climates, cold, heat, and rain": United
Farm Workers (@UFWupdates), "Ismael has been a lettuce
loader for 18 years. He shares, 'My work is very hard. We
work in different climates, cold, heat and rain. Thanks to farm
workers, the country has food. We deserve to be treated as
people, not just tools in the fields.' #WeFeedYou," Twitter,
October 13, 2022, 7:02 a.m., https://twitter.com/UFWupdates
/status/1580559635584466947.
"it will keep well for two or three weeks": Smith et al., *Leaf
Lettuce.*

"facilities spanning 4,150,000 square feet, or about ninety-five
    acres": Sysco, *2022 Annual Report*, accessed January 17, 2024,
    https://investors.sysco.com/~/media/Files/S/Sysco-IR
    /documents/annual-reports/Sysco_2022-Annual-Report
    _Web.pdf.

"returning $1.5 billion to shareholders": Sysco, *2022 Annual Report*.

"We could not have accomplished these impressive results": Sysco,
    2022 Annual Report.

"Twenty thousand pounds or say eight hundred boxes": Sysco
    Employee Reviews for Truck Driver, Indeed, accessed April
    4, 2023, https://ca.indeed.com/cmp/Sysco/reviews?fjobtitle
    =Truck+Driver.

"Over a thousand drivers and warehouse workers have gone
    on strike": Kevin Reed, "California Drivers and Warehouse
    Workers Join Strikes against Sysco in Indiana and Kentucky,"
    World Socialist Web Site, March 31, 2023, https://www.wsws
    .org/en/articles/2023/03/31/wqsk-m31.html.

"Sysco Indianapolis has implemented its contingency plans": Joe
    Schroeder, "Local Teamsters Union Strikes against Sysco,"
    Fox 59, March 27, 2023, https://fox59.com/indiana-news/local
    -teamsters-union-strikes-against-sysco.

"a recent paper put together for the UC Merced Community
    and Labor Center": Sandie Ha and Ricardo Cisneros,
    "Environmental Influences on Agricultural Worker Health,"
    UC Merced Community and Labor Center, 2022, https://clc
    .ucmerced.edu.672elmp01.blackmesh.com/sites/clc.ucmerced
    .edu/files/page/documents/environmental_influences_on
    _agricultural_worker_health.pdf.

"a three-part exposé published by *Eater*": Meghan McCarron,
    "Chef's Fable," *Eater*, July 6, 2022, https://www.eater.com
    /22996588/blue-hill-stone-barns-dan-barber-restaurant-work
    -environment-ingredients.

"the company settled a two-million-dollar class-action wage theft
lawsuit": Stefanie Tuder, "Blue Hill at Stone Barns Settles
Wage Theft Lawsuit for $2 Million," *Eater*, May 31, 2017,
https://ny.eater.com/2017/5/31/15720794/blue-hill-wage-theft
-lawsuit.

"the *New York Times* ran an exposé on Willows Inn": Julia
Moskin, "The Island Is Idyllic. As a Workplace, It's Toxic,"
New York Times, April 27, 2021, https://www.nytimes.com
/2021/04/27/dining/blaine-wetzel-willows-inn-lummi-island
-abuse.html.

"which can be a costly energy draw": Ontario's Independent
Electricity System Operator, "Leveraging Innovation to
Reduce Energy Costs," Greenhouse Canada, November 17,
2020, https://www.greenhousecanada.com/leveraging
-innovation-to-reduce-energy-costs.

"greenhouses are the largest driver of increased demand for electricity": Ontario's Independent Electricity System Operator,
"Leveraging Innovation."

"recently told the CBC that it could produce 'up to six million
bags of salad greens'": CBC News, "B.C. Vertical Farming
Company Says It Could Produce Up to 6 Million Bags of
Salad Greens a Year," April 4, 2023, https://www.cbc.ca/news
/canada/british-columbia/bc-up-vertical-farms-greens
-1.6800416.

"A 2021 paper in the journal *Resources, Conservation and Recycling*":
Tammara Soma, Rajiv Kozhikode, and Rekha Krishnan,
"Tilling Food Under: Barriers and Opportunities to Address
the Loss of Edible Food at the Farm-Level in British
Columbia, Canada," *Resources, Conservation and Recycling* 170
(July 2021), https://doi.org/10.1016/j.resconrec.2021.105571.

"organic waste represents about 40 percent of the material sent
to landfills": British Columbia, "Food and Organic Waste,"

accessed January 17, 2024, https://www2.gov.bc.ca/gov
/content/environment/waste-management/food-and-organic
-waste.

TOMATO CHUTNEY, PART II: THE EMPIRE IN A SANDWICH

"From food do all creatures come into being": As quoted in K.T.
Achaya, *Indian Food: A Historical Companion* (Delhi: Oxford
University Press, 1998).

"English cooks did tend to use spices": Marie Pellissier, "Food
in the Seventeenth Century," More Than a Kitchen Aid,
https://mediakron.bc.edu/capellmanuscript/food-in-the
-seventeenth-century-1.

"Herbs and spices were used for something like medicinal
purposes": Mark Cartwright, "The Spice Trade & the Age
of Exploration," World History Encyclopedia, June 9, 2021,
https://www.worldhistory.org/article/1777/the-spice-trade
--the-age-of-exploration/.

"Food historian Lizzie Collingham's *The Taste of Empire*": Lizzie
Collingham, *The Taste of Empire* (New York: Basic Books,
2017), 75.

"Vinegar and Sugar: The Early History": Peter J. Atkins,
"Vinegar and Sugar: The Early History of Factory-Made
Jams, Pickles, and Sauces in Britain" in *Food Industries of
Europe in the Nineteenth and Twentieth Centuries*, eds. Derek J.
Oddy and Alain Drouard (New York: Routledge, 2016), 41–54.

"placing tariffs on staple grains like wheat and corn": Katie
Carpenter, "Petitions and the Corn Laws," U.K. Parliament,
July 26, 2019, https://committees.parliament.uk/committee
/326/petitions-committee/news/99040/petitions-and-the
-corn-laws/.

"Canada, which by 1910 was the world's largest wheat exporter":
Collingham, *Taste of Empire*, 223.

"such as cauliflower leaves": Lachmi Deb Roy, "Finger Lickin'
Good: The Story of Indian Chutney," *Outlook*, November 12,
2021, https://www.outlookindia.com/magazine/story/india
-news-finger-lickin-good-the-story-of-indian-chutney
/305190.

"as British as fish and chips": Simon Majumdar, *Eating for Britain*
(London: Hodder, 2011).

"Hindoostane Coffee House in London in 1809 or 1810": 1809:
Emma Jolly, "The Hindoostane Coffee House," *London
Historians' Blog*, September 5, 2011, https://londonhistorians
.wordpress.com/2011/09/05/the-hindoostane-coffee-house/;
1810: Sejal Sukhadwala. "The Story of London's First Indian
Restaurant," *Londonist*, last updated January 31, 2019, https://
londonist.com/2016/06/the-story-of-london-s-first-indian
-restaurant.

"In *Indian Food: A Historical Companion*": Achaya, *Indian Food*,
226.

"In a *Spectator* article that makes a case for Branston Pickle":
Ameer Kotecha, "Three Cheers for Branston Pickle," *The
Spectator*, November 25, 2022, https://www.spectator.co.uk
/article/three-cheers-for-branston-pickle/.

"take you a step back in time to Granny's kitchen": Heidy Linn
McCallum, "Southern Chow Chow," *McCallum's Shamrock
Patch*, May 11, 2021, accessed via the Internet Wayback
Machine, https://web.archive.org/web/20221001050408
/https://themccallumsshamrockpatch.com/2021/05/11/southern
-chow-chow/.

BECAUSE SOMEONE SAVED THE SEED

"They sue farmers aggressively to protect their seed patents":
Paul Harris, "Monsanto Sued Small Farmers to Protect Seed
Patents—Report," *The Guardian*, February 12, 2013, https://

www.theguardian.com/environment/2013/feb/12/monsanto
-sues-farmers-seed-patents.

"Seed is life itself": The Organic & Non-GMO Report,
"Vandana Shiva and the Sacredness of Seed," April 2009,
https://non-gmoreport.com/articles/apr09/vandana_shiva
_the_sacradness_of_seed.php.

"Our mantra is that good food comes from good seed": "The
Radicle: Salt Spring Seed Sanctuary Newsletter," Summer
2022, https://seedsanctuary.com/wp-content/uploads/2022/12
/Radicle-Summer-2022.pdf.

VEGAN LEMON MACAWRONGS

"one of my favourite-ever food essays is by Jeffrey Steingarten":
Jeffrey Steingarten, "It Takes a Village to Kill a Pig," in *It
Must've Been Something I Ate* (New York: Vintage, 2002), 238.

"a recipe from the blog *Pies and Tacos*": Camila Hurst, "Lavender
Lemon Vegan Macarons," *Pies and Tacos*, April 14, 2019,
https://www.piesandtacos.com/lavender-lemon-vegan
-macarons/.

"What would disgust me as much as a raw egg white?": Kristen
Hartke, "Trust Us. You Can Use the Liquid from a Can of
Beans to Make Dessert," *The Washington Post*, October 5,
2015, https://www.washingtonpost.com/lifestyle/food/trust
-us-you-can-use-the-liquid-from-a-can-of-beans-to-make
-dessert/.

"a French macaron technique from a blog called *Bakes and
Blunders*": Colleen Gershey, "Lemon and Vanilla Macarons,"
Bakes and Blunders, https://www.bakesandblunders.com
/vegan-lemon-vanilla-macarons/.

"a blog called *Project Vegan Baking*": Tom Adams, "Vegan
Macarons," *Project Vegan Baking*, https://projectveganbaking
.com/vegan-macarons/.

"In Steingarten's boudin essay": Steingarten, "It Takes a Village," 247.

"Reading some *Serious Eats* trials": Nik Sharma, "The Science Behind Vegan Meringues," *Serious Eats*, November 17, 2022, https://www.seriouseats.com/science-of-aquafaba-meringues -5185233.

CONSIDER THE CARROT

"pollination is assisted by insects like bees, hoverflies, houseflies, and bluebottles": David Catzel, "Carrot Pollination Time," BC Seed Trials, July 22, 2018, https://www.bcseedtrials.ca /2018/07/22/carrot-pollination-time/.

"if you live within a mile or so of a plant": Dan Wyns, "Hybrid Carrot Seed Pollination," Bee Informed, September 5, 2014, https://beeinformed.org/2014/09/05/hybrid-carrot-seed -pollination-2/.

"classified as a class B noxious weed": J. Colquhoun, J.P. Fitzsimmons, and L.C. Burrill, "Wild Carrot," Oregon State University Extension Service, revised March 2003, https:// catalog.extension.oregonstate.edu/sites/catalog/files/project /pdf/pnw447.pdf.

"it's prohibited to sell or transport its seeds": Washington State Noxious Weed Control Board, Noxious Weeds Index, https://www.nwcb.wa.gov/noxious-weed-quarantine-list.

"a man who died in the 1970s": "Carrot-Juice Addiction Cited in Briton's Death," *New York Times*, February 17, 1974, accessed January 16, 2024, https://www.nytimes.com/1974/02/17 /archives/carrotjuice-addiction-cited-in-britons-death.html.

"initially domesticated in Afghanistan about five thousand years ago": John Stolarczyk, "Carrots History—The Early Years," World Carrot Museum, accessed via the Internet Wayback Machine, https://web.archive.org/web

/20220906193913/http://www.carrotmuseum.co.uk/history1
.html.

"earliest domesticated varieties were most likely purple":
Stolarczyk, "History of Carrots."

"reading extracurricular-to-museum materials": Seeds Savers
Exchange, "How to Grow Carrots (*Daucus carota*)," 2017,
https://www.seedsavers.org/site/pdf/grow-save-carrots.pdf.

"the mildly illicit novel-like baby carrot webpage": Stolarczyk,
"History of Carrots."

"baby carrots now comprise about 70 percent of carrot sales":
Canadian Food Focus, "What's in Season? Carrots," https://
canadianfoodfocus.org/in-season/whats-in-season-carrots
/#:~:text=Today%2C%2070%25%20of%20carrot%20
sales%20are%20baby%20carrots.

"the better fix would be for consumers to embrace 'ugly' produce":
Eat Grim, "Baby Carrots Are a Symptom of Our Wasteful
Food System, Not a Solution," *Medium*, August 26, 2019,
https://medium.com/eat-grim/baby-carrots-are-a-symptom
-of-our-wasteful-food-system-not-a-solution-2678504b1005.

"we do not need to physically loosen soil in order for roots to
go down and explore": Charles Dowding, "No Dig Carrots,
easier than you thought," April 16, 2021, https://youtu.be
/HCHIjxcyciY.

"growing good carrots is possible in a fresh bed like this": Charles
Dowding. "Create a no dig raised bed, compost on weeds,
with tips on planting + see the growth," April 21, 2017, https://
youtu.be/OIojWdJzoRE.

ON SUBSTITUTION

"a mixture of gluten-free flours, xanthan gum, and psyllium
husk gel to make gluten-free phyllo": Katarina Cermelj,

"Homemade Gluten Free Filo Pastry (Phyllo Dough)," *The Loopy Whisk*, January 23, 2022, https://theloopywhisk.com/2022/01/23/gluten-free-filo-pastry/.

"We can't deny the parallels our current COVID-19 pandemic shares with the Great Depression": Valerio Farris, "Water Pie Was a Depression-Era Treat—Why Are People into It Now?" *Food52*, August 20, 2021, https://food52.com/blog/26500-what-is-depression-era-water-pie.

"a water pie on TikTok": B. Dylan Hollis (@b.dylanhollis2), "WATER PIE (TikTok Vintage Recipe)," TikTok, August 31, 2023, https://www.tiktok.com/@b.dylanhollis2/video/7273706846844636459.

"peanut butter bread": CBC Radio, "Depression-Era Recipes Prove a Pandemic Hit for Toronto YouTube Chef," *As It Happens*, June 17, 2020, https://www.cbc.ca/radio/asithappens/as-it-happens-wednesday-edition-1.5615882/depression-era-recipes-prove-a-pandemic-hit-for-toronto-youtube-chef-1.5615883.

"compost soup": Kesia Kvill, Rebecca Beausaert, Maggie McCormick, and Lisa Ashton, "6 History Lessons for Eating through COVID-19 Pandemic," Arrell Food Institute, April 15, 2020, https://arrellfoodinstitute.ca/history-lessons-for-pandemic/.

"dandelion salad": Christelle Siohan, "Backyard Foraging: Dandelion Salad," *Permacrafters*, https://www.permacrafters.com/backyard-foraging-dandelion-salad/.

"sourdough bread": Emily St. James, "How to Bake Bread," *Vox*, May 19, 2020, https://www.vox.com/the-highlight/2020/5/19/21221008/how-to-bake-bread-pandemic-yeast-flour-baking-ken-forkish-claire-saffitz.

"how to avoid food waste and eat cheaply": Laken Brooks, "My Grandmother's Depression-Era Recipes Are Helping

Me Cope During Coronavirus," *Good Housekeeping*, June 8, 2020, https://www.goodhousekeeping.com/life/a32744748/coronavirus-depression-recipes/.

"bump in vegetable gardening": Marty Klinkenberg, "Seed Companies Thought Coronavirus Would Ruin Their Businesses. Instead, Demand Has Soared," *The Globe and Mail*, June 1, 2020, https://www.theglobeandmail.com/life/article-peis-veseys-sees-demand-soar-as-covid-19-spurs-vegetable-seeds-frenzy/.

"couldn't package seeds fast enough to keep up with demand": Steve Arstad, "Seeds Selling Fast as COVID-19 Era Gardeners Keep Up Planting Trend,"*iNwine*, March 21, 2021, https://infotel.ca/inwine/seeds-selling-fast-as-covid-19-era-gardeners-keep-up-planting-trend/it81663.

"it's food bank use that has increased the most": "More Canadians Are Turning to Food Banks Than Ever Before, New Report Says," CBC News, October 27, 2022, https://www.cbc.ca/news/canada/food-bank-canada-usage-1.6631120.

"A 2019 essay by Alison Herman for *The Ringer*": Alison Herman, "How NYT Cooking Became the Best Comment Section on the Internet," *The Ringer*, February 7, 2019, https://www.theringer.com/2019/2/7/18214477/nytcooking-comment-section.

"you can even forage stinging nettles": Kim Chisholm, "Stinging Nettle: Harvesting, Processing and Recipes," Wolf Camp and School of Natural Science, June 7, 2013, last updated August 24, 2020, https://www.wolfcollege.com/stinging-nettle-harvesting-processing-and-recipes/.

THE GARDEN WILL BLOOM AGAIN

"'Cúagilákv (Jess Háusti) writes about the connection between trauma": 'Cúagilákv (Jess Housty), "Winter Is for

Regeneration. The Garden's—and Yours, Too," *The Tyee*. December 14, 2021, https://thetyee.ca/Culture/2021/12/14 /Winter-Regeneration-Garden-Yours-Too/.

A FIFTY-POUND BAG OF POTATOES

"TVP, bland shelf-stable flakes patented in the 1960s": Cynthia Graber and Nicola Twilley, "Are Plant- and Fungus-Based Fake Meats Really Better Than the Real Thing?" *Gastropod*, November 24, 2021, https://gastropod.com/are-plant-and -fungus-based-fake-meats-really-better-than-the-real -thing/; Nadia Berenstein, "A Taste of Futures Past: The Rise and Fall of Spun Soy Protein," June 7, 2017, http:// nadiaberenstein.com/blog/2017/6/5/tastethefuture.

"Potatoes contain glycoalkaloids": Poison Control, "Are Sprouted Potatoes Safe to Eat?" https://www.poison.org/articles/are -green-potatoes-safe-to-eat-191.

THE SPECTACLE OF THE BIG BITE

"profiles that include a spectacle of voracious eating": Jeff Gordinier, "For Actresses, Is a Big Appetite Part of the Show?" *New York Times*, February 15, 2011, https://www .nytimes.com/2011/02/16/dining/16interview.html.

"calls out *Esquire* . . . as a particularly frequent contributor to the genre": Jeff Gordinier, "Why I'm Saying Farewell to the Best Damn Job in the World," *Esquire*, April 6, 2021, https:// www.esquire.com/food-drink/a36028763/jeff-gordinier-last -food-drinks-column/.

"more palatable to many readers than a fat woman eating in pub- lic": Haley Morris-Cafiero, "Pictures of People Who Mock Me," *Salon*, April 23, 2013, https://www.salon.com/2013/04/23 /pictures_of_people_who_mock_me/.

"the same low-calorie dinner of grilled fish and steamed vegetables": Janine Henni, "David Beckham Reveals the 'Same
Thing' Wife Victoria Has Eaten for the Last 25 Years," *People*,
February 4, 2022, https://people.com/food/david-beckham
-victoria-beckham-same-meal-eaten-25-years/.

"Fieri has convincing defenders for his long-lambasted corni-
ness": Rax King, "Love, Peace, and Taco Grease: How I Left
My Abusive Husband and Found Guy Fieri," *Catapult*, July 29,
2019, https://catapult.co/stories/love-peace-and-taco-grease
-how-i-left-my-abusive-husband-and-found-guy-fieri-by
-rax-king.

"My show has been nominated for an Emmy every single year":
David Marchese, "Padma Lakshmi Wants Us to Eat More
Adventurously," *New York Times Magazine*, August 3, 2020,
https://www.nytimes.com/interactive/2020/08/03/magazine
/padma-lakshmi-interview.html.

"something Stanley Tucci describes in an essay about Julia Child":
Stanley Tucci, "Stanley Tucci: How Julia Child Changed My
Life," *Time*, October 4, 2021, https://time.com/6103409/stanley
-tucci-taste-julia-child/.

"If a TV chef spits the food into a dump bucket": Emily Smith,
"Skinny Giada Spits Out Everything She Cooks," *Page Six*,
November 11, 2014, https://pagesix.com/2014/11/20/skinny
-giada-spits-out-everything-she-cooks/.

"'shortcuts' to 'simplify' them for white American audiences":
Nigel Ng, "Uncle Roger Found THE WORST PHO
(Rachael Ray)," October 31, 2021, https://youtu.be/bDi__5
FcebM.

"the algorithms still prioritize white creators": Janice Gassam
Asare, "Does Instagram Have a Race Problem?" *Forbes*, April 14,
2020, https://www.forbes.com/sites/janicegassam/2020/04/14
/does-tiktok-have-a-race-problem/.

"inventive vegan swaps for ingredients like anchovy paste":
Richard Makin (@SchoolNightVegan), "Looking for the
perfect Caesar salad dressing?" May 17, 2022, https://www
.instagram.com/p/CdrA8WzqioA/?hl=en.

TRIFLING

"roots in medieval custards and sixteenth-century fruit fools":
Cate Devine, "Mixing It: The English Claim It Was Their
Invention. The Scots Say It Couldn't Have Happened
Without Them. Cate Devine Goes in Search of Answers
to the Great Trifle Debate," *The Herald*, January 15, 2004,
https://www.heraldscotland.com/news/12517218.mixing
-it-the-english-claim-it-was-their-invention-the-scots
-say-it-couldnt-have-happened-without-them-cate
-devine-goes-in-search-of-answers-to-the-great-trifle
-debate/.
"following a recipe from the *Spruce Eats* called 'Classic English
Custard Sauce'": Elaine Lemm, "Classic English Custard
Sauce," *The Spruce Eats*, January 1, 2023, https://www
.thespruceeats.com/proper-custard-sauce-recipe-434930.
"A representative one of her trifle custards": Mary Berry, "Mary
Berry's Celebration Trifle," *The Mail*, December 13, 2020,
https://www.you.co.uk/mary-berry-celebration-trifle/.
"making a trifle for the TV show *Good Afternoon!*": "Mary Berry
Makes a Sherry Trifle," *Good Afternoon!*, hosted by Judith
Chalmers, first aired June 5, 1975, uploaded June 25, 2017,
https://youtu.be/3DDv7mnTagc.
"if his grandmother had wheels, she would have been a bike":
"Gino D'Acampo 'If my Grandmother had wheels she would
have been a bike' - 18th May 2010," uploaded May 18, 2020,
https://youtu.be/A-RfHC91Ewc.

"I watch Karl Clarke make a traditional sherry trifle, again for
  Christmas": "Traditional Sherry Trifle," *Ireland AM*, hosted
  Karl Clarke, Virgin Media Television, December 18, 2021,
  https://youtu.be/ix5qDbNajCk.
"I watch Nigella Lawson make an Anglo-Italian trifle": Nigella
  Lawson, "Nigella Lawson's Anglo-Italian Trifle," *Forever
  Summer with Nigella*, February 6, 2019, https://youtu.be/5Ffo
  _Rwnev8.

THE FAILURE OF THE PEPPERS

"the harmonious integration of the landscape with people":
  Brian Barth, "Permaculture: You've Heard of It, but What
  the Heck Is it?" *Modern Farmer*, April 19, 2016, https://
  modernfarmer.com/2016/04/permaculture/.

GIVE US THIS DAY OUR DAILY BEANS

"*Phaseolus vulgaris* is native to what's currently known as the
  Americas": American Indian Health and Diet Project,
  "Foods Indigenous to the Western Hemisphere," https://
  aihd.ku.edu/foods/haricot_beans.html.
"Europeans had favas and chickpeas and lentils pretty early":
  Cesare Casella's Republic of Beans, "A Selective History of
  Beans," http://www.republicofbeans.com/history.php.
"Brits eat more Heinz baked beans than anyone else": "Why
  British People Love Baked Beans," Britain Explained,
  https://britainexplained.com/why-british-people-love-baked
  -beans/.
"the dish probably emerged from similar First Nations dishes":
  "The Secret History of Baked Beans," Love Food, July 15,
  2020, https://www.lovefood.com/gallerylist/97568/the-secret
  -history-of-baked-beans.

"began producing tinned baked beans in 1895": "The Secret
History of Baked Beans."

"Heinz had made a trip to England": Thomas Farrell, "Full of
Beans: Heinz in the UK," Let's Look Again, February 16, 2015,
http://letslookagain.com/2015/02/a-history-of-heinz-in-the
-uk/.

"Tinned baked beans made it to England in 1899": Farrell,
"Full of Beans."

"1901, according to another": Teresa F. Lindeman, "Heinz Brings
Beans Back to U.S.," *Pittsburgh Post-Gazette*, January 25,
2012, https://www.post-gazette.com/business/businessnews
/2012/01/25/Heinz-brings-beans-back-to-U-S/stories
/201201250251.

"eventually the beans were adapted to suit British tastes": see
Felicity Cloake, "How to Cook the Perfect Baked Beans,"
The Guardian, May 1, 2014, https://www.theguardian.com
/lifeandstyle/wordofmouth/2014/may/01/how-to-cook
-perfect-baked-beans; "The Secret History of Baked
Beans."

"Points rationing was more flexible": Ministry of Food, "Rationing
in the United Kingdom," hand-dated December 21, 1949,
https://1940sexperiment.files.wordpress.com/2022/06/rationing
-in-the-uk.pdf.

"Tinned beans ranged in value": Ministry of Food, "Rationing
in the United Kingdom."

"The number of points citizens were allotted varied": Cook's
Info, "British Wartime Food," May 3, 2011, last updated July 11,
2022, https://www.cooksinfo.com/british-wartime-food
/#Ration_Booklets_Points.

"largest food processing plant in Europe": Business Insider,
"Inside the World's Biggest Baked Bean Factory," January 26,
2018, https://youtu.be/G6O2zTuGOVQ.

"mostly grown in Spain and Portugal": Heinz, "Tasty Tomatoes,"

accessed November 19, 2023, https://www.heinz.co.uk/
grownnotmade?category=beanz.

"veggie burgers": see J. Kenji López-Alt's technique,
which can be adapted for use with home-cooked
beans: "Really Awesome Black Bean Burgers Recipe,"
Serious Eats, last updated September 15, 2022, accessed
January 15, 2024, https://www.seriouseats.com/
the-best-black-bean-burger-recipe.

A TASTE FOR FINERY

"minimum wage for students under eighteen was $6.40 in
Ontario": Government of Ontario. Employment Standards
Act, Historical version for the period of March 1, 2005, to
September 29, 2005, accessed January 15, 2024, https://www
.ontario.ca/laws/regulation/010285/v3.

"For everyone else, $6.85": Government of Canada, "General
Hourly Minimum Wage Rates in Canada since 1965," last
updated September 12, 2022, accessed January 15, 2024,
https://srv116.services.gc.ca/dimt-wid/sm-mw/rpt2.aspx.

"in today's dollars, was $30.67 an hour": Statistics Canada,
"Employee Wages by Industry, Annual," table 14-10-0064-01,
last updated January 5, 2024, accessed January 15, 2024, https://
www150.statcan.gc.ca/t1/tbl1/en/tv.action?pid=1410006401&
pickMembers%5B0%5D=1.1&pickMembers%5B1%5D=2.2&
pickMembers%5B2%5D=3.1&pickMembers%5B3%5D=5.1&
pickMembers%5B4%5D=6.1&cubeTimeFrame.startYear=2017
&cubeTimeFrame.endYear= 2021&referencePeriods=20170101
%2C20210101.

"the living wage rate in Vancouver was $20.52 an hour":
Living Wage for Families BC, "Living Wage Rates 2021,"
November 2, 2021, https://www.livingwageforfamilies.ca
/living_wage2021.

"by 2023, it had increased to $25.68": Living Wage for Families
  BC, "Living Wage Rates 2023," November 18, 2023, https://
  www.livingwageforfamilies.ca/livingwagecalculations2023.

TWENTY-FOUR BATCHES OF ICE CREAM

"the *New York Times'* Master Ice Cream Recipe": Melissa Clark,
  "The Master Ice Cream Recipe," *New York Times*, July 1,
  2014, accessed January 15, 2024, https://www.nytimes.com
  /interactive/2014/07/01/dining/the-master-ice-cream-recipe
  .html.
"a *Serious Eats* recipe by Max Falkowitz for strawberry ice cream":
  Max Falkowitz, "The Best Strawberry Ice Cream Recipe,"
  Serious Eats, June 21, 2022, accessed January 15, 2024, https://
  www.seriouseats.com/best-strawberry-ice-cream-recipe.
"infuse my classic custard-style base with spruce tips": andrea
  bennett and Christopher Cheung, "An Ice Cream Made from
  Trees?!" *The Tyee*, June 9, 2022, https://thetyee.ca/Culture
  /2022/06/09/Ice-Cream-Made-From-Trees/.

PESTILENCE AND ABUNDANCE

"Will has written about taking care of these plants": Will
  Keats-Osborn, "Leaf Thief," *Maisonneuve*, May 8, 2018,
  accessed January 15, 2024, https://maisonneuve.org/article
  /2018/05/8/leaf-thief/.
"practising crop rotation can help guard against or suppress
  some pathogens": Margaret Tuttle McGrath, "Managing
  Plant Diseases with Crop Rotation," Sustainable Agriculture
  Research and Education, accessed January 15, 2024, https://
  www.sare.org/publications/crop-rotation-on-organic-farms
  /physical-and-biological-processes-in-crop-production
  /managing-plant-diseases-with-crop-rotation/.

"planting nitrogen fixers": "The Importance of Crop Rotation,"
   The Old Farmer's Almanac, accessed January 15, 2024, https://
   store.almanac.com/the-importance-of-crop-rotation/.
"ants, which had most likely installed the aphids on the pods":
   Ada McVean, "Farmer Ants and Their Aphid Herds,"
   McGill Office for Science and Society, May 15, 2019,
   accessed January 15, 2024, https://www.mcgill.ca/oss/article
   /did-you-know/farmer-ants-and-their-aphid-herds.

andrea bennett is a National Magazine Award–winning writer and a senior editor at *The Tyee*. Their writing has been published by *The Walrus*, *Chatelaine*, *The Atlantic*, the *Globe and Mail*, and many other outlets. Their first book of essays, *Like a Boy but Not a Boy*, was one of CBC Books' 2020 picks for the top Canadian nonfiction of the year. Originally from Hamilton, andrea is now back on the west coast after a stint in Montréal.

Entertainment. Writing. Culture. ─────────

ECW is a proudly independent, Canadian-owned book publisher. We know great writing can improve people's lives, and we're passionate about sharing original, exciting, and insightful writing across genres.

───────────────────────────── **Thanks for reading along!**

We want our books not just to sustain our imaginations, but to help construct a healthier, more just world, and so we've become a certified B Corporation, meaning we meet a high standard of social and environmental responsibility — and we're going to keep aiming higher. We believe books can drive change, but the way we make them can too.

Certified

Corporation

    Being a B Corp means that the act of publishing this book should be a force for good – for the planet, for our communities, and for the people that worked to make this book. For example, everyone who worked on this book was paid at least a living wage. You can learn more at the Ontario Living Wage Network.

This book is also available as a Global Certified Accessible™ (GCA) ebook. ECW Press's ebooks are screen reader friendly and are built to meet the needs of those who are unable to read standard print due to blindness, low vision, dyslexia, or a physical disability.

This book is printed on Sustana EnviroBook™, a recycled paper, and other controlled sources that are certified by the Forest Stewardship Council®.

FSC
www.fsc.org
MIX
Paper from
responsible sources
FSC® C103567

For every copy of this book sold, 1% of the cover price will be donated to the United Nations Relief and Works Agency (UNWRA), which provides assistance and protection for registered Palestinian refugees.

ECW's office is situated on land that was the traditional territory of many nations including the Wendat, the Anishnaabeg, Haudenosaunee, Chippewa, Métis, and current treaty holders the Mississaugas of the Credit. In the 1880s, the land was developed as part of a growing community around St. Matthew's Anglican and other churches. Starting in the 1950s, our neighbourhood was transformed by immigrants fleeing the Vietnam War and Chinese Canadians dispossessed by the building of Nathan Phillips Square and the subsequent rise in real estate value in other Chinatowns. We are grateful to those who cared for the land before us and are proud to be working amidst this mix of cultures.

ecwpress.com